DESIGN LIKE APPLE

SEVEN PRINCIPLES FOR CREATING INSANELY GREAT PRODUCTS, SERVICES, AND EXPERIENCES

JOHN EDSON

with Ernest Beck

WILEY

John Wiley & Sons, Inc.

Published by John Wiley & Sons, Inc., Hoboken, New Jersey.
Published simultaneously in Canada.

For general information on our other products and services or for technical support, please contact our Customer Care Department within the United States at (800) 762-2974, outside the United States at (317) 572-3993 or fax (317) 572-4002.

Wiley publishes in a variety of print and electronic formats and by print-on-demand. Some material included with standard print versions of this book may not be included in e-books or in print-on-demand. If this book refers to media such as a CD or DVD that is not included in the version you purchased, you may download this material at http://booksupport.wiley.com. For more information about Wiley products, visit www.wiley.com.

ISBN: 978-1-118-29031-6 (cloth)
ISBN: 978-1-118-33176-7 (ebk)
ISBN: 978-1-118-33396-9 (ebk)
ISBN: 978-1-118-33507-9 (ebk)

Printed in the United States of America

10 9 8 7 6 5 4 3 2 1

TO THE MEMORY OF AN INSANELY GREAT FAMILY
ROBERT, ANA-MARIA, SAMANTHA, AND VERONICA

ACKNOWLEDGMENTS

The principal source for what I know about design comes from an exceptionally fortunate career that I have had at LUNAR working alongside some of the most amazingly creative and brilliant people in the world of product development. Jeff Smith and Gerard Furbershaw founded and built a singular firm that is as amazing for its creative output as it is for its ability to retain employees. Few companies engender the kind of loyalty that LUNAR does, thanks to the commitment of Jeff and Gerard to an organization that values people and relationships as much as creative excellence and financial performance. I have worked for and with them for two amazing decades. Thanks, guys, for a company worth the years.

Jeff Smith also deserves credit for articulating the beauty–ingenuity–charisma framework that I write about in this book, with input and help from many superb contributors, including Prasad Kaipa, Jeff Salazar, Ken Wood, Becky Brown, Nirmal Sethia, Roman Gebhard, Matthis Hamann, and me.

My thanks to the crew of early Apple employees who helped me reconstruct the formative days of the company and the genesis of the Apple design culture: Randy Battat, Mike Looney, Clement Mok, Joy Mountford, Larry Tesler, and John Zeisler.

Special thanks to Bill Dresselhaus, one of the first product designers at Apple and a client and colleague, for his help in this effort and his interest in me and my career over the years. Many people helped me understand the design process and culture of design at Apple in more recent years, including Tony Fadell and a number of others who asked to remain anonymous.

Thanks to Josh Handy at Method Products and to Albert Shum at Microsoft for your openness in discussing what design means to your companies. Uday Dandavate helped inform and expand the ideas about design research. Thanks to John Paul for the rich discussion on managing functionality, quality, and schedule and to Ken Wood, Misha Cornes, and Nathan Shedroff for helping me frame this book and encouraging ideas along the way. Thanks to Helen Walters for motivating me to tackle this project in the first place.

This beautiful book would not have been possible without my colleagues at LUNAR who created the outstanding design, led by art director Kenny Hopper and book designer Mary Shadley. Thanks to Kevin Wong who devised the cover art concept, and to designers Anna Kwon and Gritchelle Fallesgon for collecting and creating imagery used throughout the book, and to

Carly Lane and Jonathan Cofer for the design of the project website. Danielle Guttman was invaluable in researching and coordinating a surprising array of logistics.

My writing partner, Ernest Beck, has been a crucial critic during the prototyping and refinement of this book, an optimistic guide when I've had my moments of panic, and a tolerant colleague during my eleventh hour obsessing. Thanks. And much gratitude goes to Richard Narramore and the consummate professionals at John Wiley & Sons, Inc., who entrusted me with this book and remained patient throughout the process.

To my family, friends, and colleagues, thank you for tolerating my absences, both physical and emotional, during the many hours of devotion to this project. Everyone at LUNAR has been extraordinarily supportive while carrying the extra load—and some have gone the extra mile.

Thanks to Mark Dziersk for stepping into my empty shoes and for reading the manuscript. Erik Hansen deserves a shout-out for the many years of friendship through a number of life challenges and achievements, including this project. Special thanks go to Frank and Terry for your persistent support.

This book would not have been possible without my family. For taking up the slack and for believing deeply in me, my wife and best friend, Megan, deserves the lion's share of credit and recognition for this book. I love you. Jack, for your bottomless stores of playful creativity, and Olivia, for your commitment to living life large—you are my muses and inspiration. May you each find and embrace your own creative spirit throughout your lives. And finally, thanks go to my parents for their encouragement of me to do the same.

DESIGN LIKE APPLE

Introduction

Apple, design, and Steve Jobs.

It's safe to say that you have probably had a firsthand experience with an Apple product or service—and that you have had a deeper experience over the past three decades with a succession of products created by one of the world's most valuable companies. It's also safe to say that you have visited an Apple Store—many times perhaps, to buy or browse or just to gawk in wonder—or have logged onto the Apple website.

If you're like many people, you talk about the product, whether a Mac, an iPod, an iPhone, or an iPad, and the experience with Apple itself as if they were an important relationship. There is a reason for that.

Whether you're a trained creative professional or someone without even a passing interest in the world of design, you will have noticed that everything Apple does has an approachable simplicity and purity that sets it apart from most other technology companies in the world. There is a discipline and consistency in everything Apple creates and a relentless drive toward innovation. How iPads or iPhones function and interact with the user, and how easily they operate, is just as noteworthy as the refined look, the attention to details, and the touchability of their surfaces. For all this, you can blame design.

The iPhone 4S brought voice recognition and smarts to life through Siri—another Apple innovation that makes technology feel more human. *Image: Apple Inc.*

In other words, what you are experiencing when you turn on your iPhone is the power of design. You can see and experience design in the product, and, as I will explain in this book, you will see and experience design in the company itself. Design is everywhere at Apple and infused in its culture. From his earliest days at Apple, Steve Jobs set the standard that all products should be "insanely great." For me, as a designer and a customer, that means these products always embody the highest level of performance, function, and beauty. Then they reach an even higher rung of achievement: they go beyond simple sufficiency to the realm of surprise and delight.

It is easy to draw a direct line linking Apple's tenacious commitment to design and its unparalleled commercial and financial success. Great products boost the bottom line. But it's also important to go deeper to examine the design processes and practices that Apple uses in its management and organization. By exploring the strategic role that design plays in Apple's corporate culture and structure, I will make observations and extract key insights that business leaders and designers from any industry can use.

If you're a manager with a business degree and haven't had too much interaction with the concept of design or with your company's design department—if there is one, that is—you might be thinking that this book isn't for you. I would argue otherwise. Design isn't just a discipline taught in design schools. It isn't a tool or strategy unique to Steve Jobs or to Apple or to design firms. You might not realize it, but design infuses just about everything we interact with, from toothbrushes to clothes and cars and computers. In that sense, design is part of the material world and myriad products and services that companies create and that we buy. Some companies have used design from the very beginning, whereas others have discovered design along the way and have integrated design into their culture even after management structures and operational frameworks have been established.

In my mind, design is more than just the way a product looks or functions. It is a way of thinking about the world and how it works. By utilizing the main elements of design and how designers think, any company can leverage design the way Apple does. I know this is possible because as the front man for my internationally recognized global design firm, LUNAR, I speak with hundreds of businesspeople every year about how to grow their companies with innovative and exciting new products and services. More precisely, I speak with them about the future. Inevitably, these discussions about the future lead to design.

"We want to be the Apple of our industry."

Over the past two decades, the increased focus on design in the popular media and culture and in business and management schools has drawn attention to how exceptional design can help companies exceed their corporate goals, even if the company doesn't have a history of design or its management doesn't have a design background. I see this shift in thinking every time a business leader looks me in the eye and emphatically tells me, "We want to be the Apple of our industry."

I hear that all the time. But what does it really mean?

Sometimes, even savvy managers have only a vague notion of what design is, and that is often rooted in a number of myths about Apple's corporate design culture. Design and the broader creative approach go way beyond cool products that consumers find addictive. Apple sees design as a tool for creating beautiful experiences that convey a coherent point of view down to the smallest detail—from the tactile feedback of a keyboard to the out-of-the-box experience when a customer opens an iPhone or an iPad package. Much attention has been focused on those packages because design at Apple is part of a continual company-wide innovation process that doesn't stop at the design studio door. As I explain in this book, when design is the foundation and essential component of everything a company does, the package is as important as everything else.

Apple isn't the only company that has so passionately embraced design. It is a great example but not the only one. Design is happening at companies in every conceivable industry and sector. I see design becoming part of the conversation everywhere I look and not just at our firm or at the Stanford design program where I teach or because I am a designer. I hear design talked about in corporate boardrooms and among strategists and product development departments whether the company makes automotive parts or scooters for kids or video games.

Today, companies realize that in a competitive global marketplace it is imperative to know much more than which styling features or color options will make their product more admired and desired by customers. Executives are coming around to the idea that they must create experiences and meaning that go beyond the product. To me, this is clear evidence that the influence of design is expanding and changing as managers accept that operational excellence is not the only way to grow a business. They see that design is not an afterthought but rather a way to differentiate their products from those of competitors. They understand that what you really need is a better product rather than more ads or a more famous or notorious celebrity pitch person.

My interest in design dates from my youth. My father was an engineer for General Electric, and my mother was a math major with a great interest in the arts. Because of their influence, I felt equally comfortable in a science museum or an art museum. I have always spanned these two worlds—or, as Jobs described it at the launch of the original iPad, the intersection of Liberal Arts Street and Technology Street—in my professional and personal lives and in private pursuits.

This merging of the creative and the analytical, the artistic and the technical, is a theme that has followed me to this day. I studied mechanical engineering at the University of Texas at Austin, but after working for a couple of years in this field I knew that a purely technical career wasn't enough for me. So I enrolled in Stanford University's Joint Program in Design, so called because it was truly a collaborative effort sponsored by the departments of mechanical engineering and art.

Since graduating in 1993, I have had the great fortune to teach a number of classes in product design, the undergraduate version of my graduate studies. I love teaching creativity to some of the smartest students in the world, who have spent much of their time focusing on critical rather than creative thinking. The coursework in the program should not be confused with an industrial design program. It is rooted in engineering while also giving students the tools to explore creative alternatives. It teaches them how to prototype in a workshop with machine tools and laser cutters and also to appreciate aesthetics. Many of these ideas and concepts about the coming together of liberal arts and technology and its impact on design are discussed in this book.

Demand for this program at Stanford has grown dramatically over the past years. More than ever, students are aware of design as an academic and career pursuit much earlier in their lives. Perhaps this is why you picked up this book. As a culture, we are thinking, talking, and writing about design in new and exciting ways.

In fact, you'd be hard-pressed to buy anything today that hasn't been designed—or at least intentionally considered—even if not to the highest standards. Looking for a vegetable peeler? What was once an undifferentiated bent-metal tool is now available in a wide range of colors and materials, each with its own take on providing more comfort and status to the customer. The fact is that good design has led to products that change the way we see the world and interact with it.

Because of this increased awareness of design, companies are looking to design to augment their competitive advantage, and they are looking to design firms to help them. We speak with clients about their products and potential products, and we listen to their stories and figure out which design strategies might better express their brand voice, solve their technical challenges, and connect on a deeper level with their customers. My main motivation in writing this book is to help businesspeople codify the advice we provide to our clients every day and to help designers understand how to broaden their roles inside business. Much of what you will read here is based on the insights and experiences gleaned from my involvement in the design world, working with many different clients, as well as my experiences interacting directly with Apple and interviews with Apple veterans and industry leaders in design and technology.

Throughout the book I talk generally about "managers" and "designers" as if they were always separate and entirely distinct categories within an organization. I do this for efficiency's sake, as a kind of shorthand, because in fact I know many managers who are incredibly creative, and I've also encountered many designers and creative types who run thriving and profitable businesses. But as a rule, when I talk about managers, they are leaders from strategy, marketing, engineering, and operations who have demanding roles that traditionally lean heavily on analytical capabilities. By contrast, when I speak of designers, I more likely think of people whose talents and roles are grounded more in creative strategies and solutions.

In this book, I use my experience as a design professional to unravel how Apple and other companies use design to their best advantage and how Apple and other companies sometimes fail to do so (yes, even Apple can falter)—and why. I want you to come away from reading this book with a good idea of what design is and what it can do for you and your organization. I provide a series of management tips and advice to help you steer your organization in the direction of design or bolster an existing design capability to its fullest potential.

I hope readers will be intrigued and inspired to apply these lessons at their own businesses, regardless of their positions in their organizations. I wrote this book to champion design and to encourage everyone in an organization to appreciate the power of design and to use it as Steve Jobs did at Apple—to create "insanely great" products and attain outrageous business results.

Design Makes All the Difference

Beauty, ingenuity, and charisma create a unique competitive advantage.

The lesson to be learned from Apple's approach to design and its integration into the corporate culture is that design can make an enormous difference to a business. Apple is among a small number of public companies that have enthusiastically embraced design and invested in it as the single most important differentiating characteristic in their products and services. Design means that Apple products are unique and stand out in a crowd, from the minimalist styling and metal and glass enclosures to the seamless and fluid functioning of the software.

What do we really mean when we say *design*? The word is often used to describe many things. I think of design as both a process and an outcome. As a process, design is a verb, or how an object was created. As an outcome, design is a noun, the object itself, such as a computer or a lamp or a sofa. I'd like to add another meaning: Design as an experimental mindset, a way of thinking about things that culminates in a fresh approach or in something new or innovative. Because Apple uses this full-court design approach to create its amazing products, I want to talk about the process and the outcomes to help you understand how to leverage design in your own work. First, let's break down the outcomes of Apple's design and development process into three elements—beauty, ingenuity, and charisma—and use them as lenses to consider and evaluate your own company's products and services.

There may be no better industry to illustrate how design makes a difference than the dynamic cell phone sector and the rise and fall of three of its battling handset titans: Motorola, Nokia, and Apple. Designers empathize with me when I relate this story about the different approaches to design that these companies used, and it's a great tale to get you thinking about the central role of design in bringing successful products to market.

"Good news," said the engineering manager at Motorola proudly one day in the late 1990s when my firm was working with the company on designing a new family of cell phones. "We are going to use the same base for both phones," he told me. "We'll be able to save millions in manufacturing." At hearing these words my first thought was, yes, this is good news for him, the guy in charge of engineering. But for me it was a stark reminder of how little Motorola truly valued design. This decision signaled that the company was making another decision concerning product development based on elevating engineering and cost savings over design and striving for a result that would entice and delight customers.

But let's step back for a moment and look at the history to see how we got to that fateful moment.

At the time, LUNAR was working with Motorola to create new cell phone designs based on its then successful StarTAC platform, which was a slim, lightweight flip phone popular with mobile professionals. Motorola wanted to build on that success and attract a new and more diverse group of customers to its brand. Creating phone designs with different appearances—what we in the industry call "aesthetic expressions"—was a way to extend the brand to a wider audience, or so the thinking went at the time.

The Talkabout phone was an early step by Motorola to design products with more consumer appeal, though it lacked Apple-like commitment to making a stand out statement. *Image: LUNAR*

This design initiative came at the tail end of a much larger design strategy project that led to a vision for four unique brands targeting different consumer segments. LUNAR assembled a team of researchers to examine global consumer lifestyles and preferences, and from there we devised a set of design principles for the four consumer segments Motorola was trying to capture. This is one important aspect of a designer's job: to strategize with companies about their once and future products before actually going to the studio to design the products.

A suite of conceptual designs emerged from this process that embodied the varying principles or design language that would define the subbrands. These were early prototypical designs that would later be used as inspirations for a team of designers to create actual phones in harmony with the four design languages. This design strategy lets you coordinate the look and characteristics of an entire family of products, like Motorola's StarTAC line.

Once the design language was defined, we then applied those attributes to a version of the StarTAC phone called Talkabout, which targeted a customer group we were calling Active Networkers—those people who wanted a phone to connect to family and friends but who weren't especially interested in technology or extra gizmos. We gave this phone simple contemporary styling and fun colors like bright ocean blue. In parallel to our efforts, Motorola's internal team designed a version of the phone for another brand called Timeport, which had a trim look and silvery tones and was aimed at more demanding mobile professionals.

Because the guts for the all the phones were identical, the engineering manager I spoke with realized that he could save Motorola a ton of money by building just one version of the base of the flip phone. This base would be paired to either the Talkabout top or the Timeport top. The base remained the same, but the top changed. It had one body with a number of different heads, which is why I call this a Frankenstein approach to product design. And, like Frankenstein the monster, some of the phones looked a bit off: The head didn't fit the body.

Motorola created a Frankenstein phone because it regarded design as a marketing add-on. Its culture dictated that engineering decisions take top priority, sometimes at the expense of wowing customers. The customers wanted phones that were easy to use, that reflected their personality, and that had features meaningful to them. Even changing the outsides or the skins only vaguely addressed the desire for individual style.

Apple, by contrast, creates designs that have a deep and uncompromising aesthetic, unlike Motorola's ability to create a last-minute mash-up of a product.

This is not to say that I'm naive about the kind of pressures Motorola was facing and that confront every modern business. I know that the four C's—cost, competition, customers, and capability—weigh on an organization and its leadership on a daily basis, and that it's crucial to run an operational business that is attentive to all these factors. In that sense, the decision by the Motorola engineering manager was incredibly smart when considering the cost dimension. But what about the customer dimension? Motorola's engineering culture supported measurable, analytical decision making that favored bottom-line efficiencies above all else. Unfortunately, that orientation alone cannot produce products that captivate customers.

In contrast to this type of practice, Apple has a top-line orientation that leads to premium products with high profit margins that can be reinvested in development. I spoke about this with Tony Fadell, a former Apple executive who led the development of the iPod and the iPhone. "Everyone goes for market share, but Apple goes for margin," Fadell told me. "We were happy to have a smaller percentage of the mobile phone market with iPhone because we made a higher percentage of the profit. And with all that money, you can invest in making the next great product."

Having worked with Apple for many years as an outside design consultant, and through my conversations with former Apple engineers, I know that at Apple design is king. Creating products that rise to the level of insanely great is paramount to everything else. You can see this in a phone that feels like a solid piece of glass, or in a laptop computer that has backlit keys, or in a mouse with a touch-sensitive surface. In all these products, the cost dimension isn't allowed to overrun the design considerations. As an Apple engineer said to me, "Cost is for operations to figure out. Our job is to create the right product."

THE SIREN SONG OF TECHNOLOGY

There is another aspect of this epic tale of cell phone giants that sheds light on design and technology and how they impact each other.

Engineering invention and ingenuity has driven much of Motorola's success since it was founded in 1928 as Galvin Manufacturing Corporation. In 1930, Galvin introduced the Motorola radio, one of the first commercially successful car radios. This was just the beginning for a company whose talented engineers would later produce the world's first commercial cellular device, among many other innovations. Creative engineering also led the company to the StarTAC, a phone that was ahead of its time in terms of size and weight. Although I disagreed with the engineer in charge about the decision to make Frankenstein phones, Motorola's engineering prowess is among the most impressive in the business, and that capability resulted in many outstanding products. One of these products was a phone called the RAZR V3—a complete reinvention of the flip phone expression. Introduced in 2004, it featured a surprisingly

slim profile and a brushed metal housing that conveyed a sensual and sophisticated look customers loved.

Yet the RAZR V3's beautiful shell hid a nagging problem that was rooted in Motorola's failure to incorporate design into its development process: The underlying user interface hadn't been revamped. I have always found this puzzling, because this situation created a disconnect between the phone's great looks and how it functioned. To understand how real people valued the appearance of the phone compared to its ease of use (what designers call *usability*), I created an informal, ad hoc research project.

"How do you like your phone?" I would randomly ask anyone whom I saw with a RAZR V3 in hand. An overwhelming majority of these people would look down at their phone, spin it in their hand, and say, "I love it!" Then I would ask, "What's it like to use?" The reaction was quite different. Frowns and complaints followed. Unprompted, a few people even showed me how hard it was to look up a phone number. What had gone wrong? My assessment is that Motorola's RAZR V3 used design on the surface to great success, but had not gone deeper to implement better design at all levels. The company was still making crucial decisions based on an engineering sensibility and operational limitations. The company's interface designers were saddled with an old operating system because management wouldn't make the investment to switch the brains of the phone to match the outstanding body.

In parallel to Motorola's cell phone problems, the Finnish company Nokia had gained fame and a global market by designing phones that resonated with customers on all levels. Unlike Motorola, the user interfaces on Nokia's phones were easy to navigate, and what's more the company was offering stylish handsets that were more like a personal accessory than an electronic device. Needless to say, customers loved everything about their Nokia phones.

Motorola's RAZR V3 made an impact with its slimness and ingenious use of materials but fell short of creating a lasting impression because of its clunky interface.

Behind the scenes, another force was at work. Nokia was building phones based on newer digital transmission technology, while Motorola was standing by the older analog technology. Motorola's engineering leadership argued that analog was the way to keep going, because it offered the lowest-cost manufacturing and that, as a result, analog would win out. But Nokia rightly believed that digital would eventually empower all kinds of desirable services on the phone and that it would ultimately lead the way to richer customer experiences with the phone, such as the ubiquitous Internet-enabled smartphones we see today. Nokia also knew that initially, digital offered longer battery life, a feature that end user's would value highly. Nokia was right in the short term and also in its long-term hunches. It was an obvious decision in retrospect, but the basis for it is durable: Nokia was investing in what customers cared about rather than which technology was incumbent. The right design approach is to put the customer— not the technology or the company's operational capabilities—in the center of the development environment. Use the customer as the guide and the audience for everything. Nokia was living up to its tagline: Connecting People.

Too often, companies like Motorola look at their technology base as the source for what they can make. In other words, they are following the siren song of technology and deploying design in only a partial way. The result is therefore only partially successful—in blips, you could say. The StarTAC was ingenious in its use of technology. Blip. The RAZR V3 leveraged that ingenuity and added a sleek beauty. Blip, blip. Motorola's adoption of the Android operating system on phones that leverage their engineering capabilities points to a company that has learned to use design to connect with customers.

Apple's iPhone did all these things from the start. It is one of those products that come along every now and then to change an industry and the way we live. At the heart of this change was how Apple used design to rethink what a phone is and what it can deliver. First, Apple engineers created a physical design that attracted us. Then they brought technology in line with how they wanted people to experience it. Through the simple software, the model of useful little apps, and the whole Apple brand experience, iPhone bonded with customers and created an in-depth connection. In sum, I see how Apple used design to create a product with *beauty, ingenuity,* and *charisma.* These three qualities can result only when you are committed to creating *extreme emotional engagement* through the design of your products.

Apple used design to create a product with *beauty, ingenuity,* and *charisma.* These three qualities can result only when you are committed to creating *extreme emotional engagement* through the design of your products.

You might think that extreme emotional engagement is something that just happens spontaneously or by chance, like falling in love. Is it possible to intentionally design something like a cell phone so that it generates an emotional response? Cognitive scientist Don Norman writes in his book *Emotional Design* that there are three emotional processes at work when we encounter the world around us: behavioral, visceral, and reflective. We're always sizing up things in the world to determine whether they might be useful, comfortable, delicious, desirable, puzzling, funny, or any of a thousand other descriptions. And we're continuously shifting between the three different emotional modes in concert with the things and situations we encounter.[1] Norman argues that a product triggers emotional responses, and whether we pay attention or not depends on our fight-or-flight responses. If you're aware of this connection and use design skillfully, you can invoke these trigger responses.

At LUNAR, we occasionally go through an exercise to make sure that our creative juices keep flowing. It's called Moonshine, but doesn't involve bootleg booze. We believe it's crucial for creative people to have the time and space sometimes to exercise their creative muscles, to look outside the challenges posed by our clients, and to develop their own ideas. This way, they are stimulated to explore any number of new ways of applying design. Fascinated by Norman's academic description of how the design of an object can connect emotionally, we enlisted the Moonshine tradition to create a response to his book.

Our designers posed a range of questions to try our hand at isolating the three responses in people, and we settled on focusing on three: 1 What if we just admitted that the chair we have in the bedroom is for holding dirty clothes instead of for sitting? 2 What would a trash can look like if it were designed to make you want to throw things into it? 3 How could we transform the most mundane household object into sculpture?

Our Moonshine experiment led to some interesting results that we believe validated Norman's cognitive framework. The Hanger Chair, as we call it, is evocative of a chair, but it is clearly more useful for hanging clothes. Playing with the icon of a chair and the wire hanger, this design forces the viewer into a reflective mode. The Trash Hole is a wastebasket that creates an inviting target and urges you to hit the basket with that crumpled-up paper. A sink stopper we jokingly called Water Stopping Water reinterprets the conventional household product by borrowing the form from a water droplet frozen in midsplash.

We asked ourselves a number of questions about these products. What emotional responses do you encounter when you look at these concepts? Does the Hanger Chair make you laugh because of the way it visually pokes fun at your messy habit? Is the Trash Hole engaging your desire to play a game and tempting you

The Trash Hole plays with the idea of the conventional trash can, making the target opening vertical. *Image: LUNAR*

This concept for a sink stopper uses design to surprise us, transforming a mundane object into sculpture. *Image: LUNAR*

The Hanger Chair resembles the side chair we all have in our bedrooms, but acknowledges its real purpose: temporarily storing clothes. *Image: LUNAR*

to throw something through its target? Does Water Stopping Water make you smile because it has managed to freeze water in midsplash? These are the kinds of questions and responses that design can engender.

All of these ideas are striking because they stand out from the usual and connect to the customer in an unusual way. Nancy Duarte, a consultant who helps corporate leaders create compelling and persuasive presentations through the lens of storytelling, says in her book *Resonate* that because so many products are similar, "the one that makes an emotional connection wins."[2] Let's look at how extreme emotional engagement shows up in Apple designs.

BEAUTY

It's an old cliché but still true: You have only one chance to make a great first impression. When customers first encounter your product, service, or experience, they will size it up first for its aesthetic attractiveness. Do they find it beautiful, sophisticated, cute, novel, or serious in the way it looks or feels? This is not an exhaustive list, but the point here is that the aesthetic attributes of a product matter in the way that we perceive it. And whether or not you pay attention to it, the *expression* of your products will elicit an emotional response in the people you're trying to attract. We can think of the term *beauty* as a way to refer to any extreme emotional engagement created by the aesthetic attractiveness of a product.

One day I bumped into a friend and noticed she had a new Hewlett-Packard notebook computer featuring graphic patterns that LUNAR had helped design. I shared with her some of the backstage stories about how those beautiful graphics found their way into the computer—the months of work developing a graphic pattern, working with manufacturers to reproduce the pattern faithfully and beautifully, and making adjustments to the pattern to account for the technical aspects of tooling. She was amazed.

"Why go to all that trouble just for a PC, something that I buy solely for its function?" she wondered aloud. When I asked her about what her checklist included when she set out to buy a PC, we ended up talking about her technical requirements. But when I asked her why she chose HP, her answer was short and to the point. "Because it looks so cool," she responded.

Clearly, it was worthwhile for HP to have invested in the design of the patterns, because it created an extreme emotional engagement in a world of exceptionally similar offerings. Motorola's RAZR V3 did the same thing: It had beauty. It tapped into this human response and by so doing broke the mold for a cell phone. The RAZR V3's amazing thinness and extraordinary metal finish surprised us. We marveled at the surfaces and stopped to think about how all that technology fit into such a slim package. We couldn't help but touch it to see how it felt and to explore how those buttons managed to give a satisfying click feedback even though they were so impossibly thin.

Apple understands these principles and uses design to trigger our emotional reactions in dozens of ways. Consider these three dominant design cues in the Apple products you've seen and might even have in your possession:

Thin. In products of all kinds (and especially in technology products), thin profiles where we might otherwise expect a thick one surprise and attract us. Engineers work hard to pack electronics into very slim packages—and designers support that effect with illusions in the design. The bright metal band around the iPhone 4 and 4S masks the true overall thickness of the phone, just like the flat edge on the MacBook Pro gives the impression that it represents the total thickness of the machine,

Whether or not you pay attention to it, the expression of your products will elicit an emotional response in the people you're trying to attract.

These HP notebooks use beautiful graphic patterns to differentiate from their competition, skillfully elevating technology products to an emotional purchase. *Image: LUNAR*

even though the product bulges out to a dimension that can fit all of the electronics. The backs of the iPad 2 and its successor use a tapering effect that thins out to a knife-edge to achieve the same impression.

Tactile. Apple pays close attention to how its products feel, both physically and virtually. The widespread use of metal and glass enhances that solid feel to convey the impression that it is one solid thing rather than a box wrapped around a bunch of components. On the screen, we are delighted by how the user interface has been designed to move and transform like objects in the real world. For example, when an application is minimized, it becomes a fluid shape that appears to get sucked down into an icon at the bottom of the screen. This offers a visual cue so that we know where to find it again. As humans, we are highly sensory, so these design attributes help us relate to the technology in a beautiful way.

Simple. Apple's single most defining designer attribute is simplicity. The forms of every Apple product are geometric, symmetrical, and aligned to create a purity that is hard to copy. The mouse with only one button. The track pad with no apparent buttons. The bottom of the laptop that is stripped of all the clutter often found there in competitors' products. Even the product labels that are required by law are silkscreened onto housings in a type so faint it is hard to read with the naked eye. On my MacBook Pro, the edges of the keyboard align with the width of the screen hinge and also align, amazingly, with the width of the page in my word processing software. This simplicity touches everything that Apple designs, including the retail stores, which make me feel like I've walked into a contemporary art museum. In 2011, I was in the Apple Store in the Stanford Shopping Center in California that had a lighting effect on the ceiling that was incredibly even. I couldn't figure out how light reflected onto

Apple designers maximize a perception of thinness in the MacBook Pro by emphasizing a thin belt of aluminum and by hiding the remaining thickness in a tapered shape on the bottom.
Image: Apple Inc.

that surface so cleanly—until I realized that the entire ceiling was a translucent panel and the lighting was coming from above it. You could say, well, why bother with such design details when you're only selling a computer? But it's the attention to all of these details that together support Apple's commitment to beauty.

INGENUITY

Apple's iPhone 4S is a beautiful object. You hold it in your hand and marvel at its solid feel and glossy surface. And when you turn it on you recognize something else: its ingenuity. You hear the built-in voice-recognition system called Siri, which is ready to help you with any question, almost as if you had the concierge at a Four Seasons Hotel always available in your pocket. Ingenuity goes beyond mere invention. It's the way in which smarts—often technical and natural—are applied to solve problems in ways that amaze, surprise, and delight us. It's the way that complexity becomes simple elegance in the hands of a customer to create extreme emotional engagement.

Plenty of companies pour money into research and development, just like Apple does. But there are some hallmarks of the Apple approach that put technology in a place to really make a difference. The kind of invention that Apple uses qualifies as ingenious innovation. It's the kind of innovation that creates value for people and helps companies capture that value. In big ways and small, Apple's products embody ingenuity.

Ingenuity doesn't always depend on a new supporting technology. Sometimes ingenious solutions come from applying existing components in new ways. The breakthrough of the iPod was that Apple stitched together the bits and pieces that other MP3 players were using into a system that people understood.

Consider some of the ways that Apple has delivered ingenuity in its products:

Human. Apple prizes making complex technology conform to the way that humans naturally work with the world. The handwriting technology behind (the failed) Newton personal digital assistant and the (more successful) voice recognition concierge Siri are perfect examples. Siri is a complex system working behind the scenes that makes interacting with a phone more like a human interaction, as well as easier and even fun. The gestural inputs that Apple is teaching us on the iPhone and other devices taps into our extraordinarily sophisticated hands. As Steve Jobs put it when addressing the 1997 World Wide Developers Conference, "You've got to start with the customer experience and work back toward the technology."[3]

Craft. Much of Apple's ingenuity shows up in the execution and delivery of the beautifully crafted final product. Most manufacturers try to create designs that will accommodate the manufacturing tooling; Apple has always looked at tooling as a means to the right end. Traditionally, plastic enclosures for electronics products have side surfaces that are slightly angled. This angle is a requirement of the way that the molds for plastic parts are made most cheaply. But to the trained eye, that small angle is visible. When Apple wanted plastic computer cases with perfectly perpendicular sides, more expensive tooling was required. Apple's priority is creating an end product that embodies the vision. It doesn't tailor the vision for the conveniences of the manufacturing processes.

Elegance. At every turn, Apple solves problems simply, or at least the solutions appear to be simple, although the reality is that a great deal of effort is put into making it seem that way. That's elegance: simple solutions for complex problems. Other computer makers build latches in their laptops to hold the screen closed against the keyboard, but Apple was the first company to engineer a complex hinge that employs cams and springs to hold the screen shut. Those mechanisms are perfectly tuned to be strong enough to keep the screen closed but also weak enough to allow you to open them without lifting the bottom half of the laptop in the process.

The lesson here is that you have to strive for more than just technical excellence and invention. Never fall in love with technology for technology's sake; technology is merely a means to creating incredible utility that appeals to people. This is a common problem in Silicon Valley: entrepreneurs create a new technology and believe that there will be an instant market for it. As these stories suggest, when technology is coupled with innovation and great design, winning products are the result.

> Never fall in love with technology for technology's sake; technology is merely a means to creating incredible utility that appeals to people.

Another company that effectively deploys design and ingenuity is Method Products, the San Francisco–based maker of home-care and personal products, from laundry detergents to hand soaps to sanitizers. It's certainly not a high-tech company, but Method is always looking for ways to marry technology with design and innovation to entice the consumer to reach for its products. In this case, they are cleaning products, where innovation is subtle and aimed directly at responding to basic human needs to keep clothes and our bodies clean.

Consider laundry detergent. Since its founding a decade ago, Method has made advances in this category by questioning industry assumptions. In 2004, Method launched a laundry detergent with a three-times-concentrated liquid that enabled the company to shrink the package by one-third, which saved on the use of plastic, transportation costs, and water (which is the main

The Method Laundry Detergent bottle brings ingenuity to a daily chore. Highly concentrated detergent means less packaging waste, and the one-handed pump action eliminates messy drips. *Image: Method*

ingredient in most laundry detergents). A concentrated detergent also played into Method's commitment to sustainability and, in turn, made retailers happy because they could save on shelf space.

But with an Apple-like drive toward ingenuity, Method wanted to go further with the concept of a concentrated detergent. It developed an eight-times-concentrated detergent. The problem, however, was how to dispense the plant-based liquid detergent, because existing delivery devices didn't fit the technological advance. Method experimented with soluble pellets, a delivery system that had always dogged detergent manufacturers, because pellets don't always dissolve completely. "We were left with a concentrated form but no way to deliver it," recalls Joshua Handy, Method's vice president of industrial design and innovation.

After several years and much tinkering and experimentation, the idea surfaced for a pump bottle dispenser. This would give consumers an easy and accurate way to dose the amount of detergent needed "even while blindfolded and holding a baby," Handy jokes. It would also solve the big problem of overdosing while ensuring that the detergent got where it was supposed to go and dissolved properly. Ingenious.

Now let me tell you a story about how ingenuity sometimes doesn't work. A novel technology doesn't always mean it's an ingenious product. Just because you have a patent for a great new technology doesn't mean you have a product. Take robots. In 1999, an inventor who had built a residential robot prototype came calling at LUNAR for help. He wanted the robot, which he claimed could do household chores and even fetch beers from the fridge, to be prepped for commercial delivery.

Everyone loves robots. Ever since Isaac Asimov wrote about them in the 1950s, robots have captured our collective imagination about what the future holds. And this inventor had certainly captured

my attention. Nonetheless, I had some important questions to ask, like the ones I always ask potential clients at the start an engagement—factual stuff that helps me to understand where our firm could best be of service. Does your prototype work? What are your projected costs, and who is your target buyer? What is the business model and value proposition? By the time we'd asked the last question, the robot inventor was exceptionally frustrated. He didn't have sufficient answers, and he cut off the conversation. "I am looking for a firm that just gets it," he fumed.

Like many inventors, this guy was blinded, I think, by the siren song of the technology. Yet, as with a lot of technology that we can easily envision as the next big thing, robots have always been just around the corner. This inventor was angry because he couldn't answer my questions about the product. I suspect he assumed my queries were getting in the way of his quest to equip every home in America with a walking, talking household helper, when in fact I was hoping to help steer his passion toward something that would be meaningful to people rather than being merely a novelty.

Willow Garage is another company with a gang of technologists who are pursuing the illusive robotic future. Founded in 2006 and based in Menlo Park, California, in the heart of Silicon Valley, Willow Garage uses a crowdsourcing approach to technology development. This company has created a personal robot that rolls around on wheels and is packed full of sensors and has arms and interchangeable "hands" for a variety of tasks. Sounds promising. Yet Willow Garage hasn't clearly defined what the robot is good at, nor is the company programming it for specific tasks. Instead, the idea is to form a community of researchers and developers who will create programs—apps, if you will—for the robot. This is an open-sourced platform approach to technology development that might just uncover the killer application for a domestic robot.

In its search for the killer app for robots, Willow Garage is opening up the challenge to a broad community with its Personal Robot 2—a platform for experimentation and innovation.
Image: Willow Garage

In 2011, Willow Garage spun off a company called Suitable Technologies to focus on building robots that will serve as remote avatars for people working away from their office who want to get more of the intangible benefits that come from being there in person. Armed with a camera, screen, speakers, and a microphone, these robots are essentially rolling videoconferencing machines, driven around by employees working from a remote location. The premise is that when you can't be in your office, you miss out on face-to-face interactions and bumping into people in the hallway. Without being there in the room, you can't turn to face people when you talk to them. This robot promises to be our surrogate body carrying our head, eyes, and ears around wherever we want to go.

While it's fun to think about the future of the workplace with this kind of technology, I wonder if these inventions will have staying power once the novelty wears off. Even more, I wonder how we might use different technology—perhaps nonrobotic technology—to design even better connections between people than are achievable by mimicking human movements with a surrogate robot. For example, if screen and camera combos became prolific in a building, and especially in conference rooms, I could "attend" more than one meeting at a time without having to drive a robot between them.

The search for an ingenious application of robotic technology for the home or office continues, and the open-source approach of Willow Garage is widening that search. But it's not pure invention that constitutes problem solving that makes a difference. Real ingenuity is a clever, brilliant solution that surprises us by how simply and naturally it caters to our needs.

CHARISMA

We often say that politicians are popular because they have charisma, that certain spark of charm and attractiveness.

We also know when they don't have charisma because we see they can't relate or connect to the public in an easy and natural way. Something is missing. In that sense, you could say that charisma is the sum total of the great experiences surrounding politicians, be it their hair and ambiance, their personal story and family, and of course their policies. Charisma is a feeling you get from this person. The same is true of products and companies.

Charisma is the positive characteristic of the very best companies that creates an extreme emotional engagement for customers. Products and services exhibit charisma when they consistently behave in a way that demonstrates an interest in me and my needs and, at the same time, exhibit what I call a leadership personality. These can be small things, as when my Wells Fargo ATM learns my behaviors and offers me meaningful shortcuts to improve banking services. Or for larger reasons, as when I urge friends to stay at Ace Hotels because they offer a charismatic experience, which has converted me from a customer into an advocate for the brand. That is the power of charisma.

> **Products and services exhibit charisma when they consistently behave in a way that demonstrates an interest in me and my needs and, at the same time, exhibit what I call a leadership personality.**

Politicians make you feel that you are the center of the universe, and great products do, too. But it can be tough for companies to erase a long-standing charisma deficit—even if they come up with a winning product. That's what happened to Microsoft in 2006 after it finally launched its version of a portable music player called Zune a full six years after Apple revolutionized the industry with the iPod. Being so late to the party, it wasn't at all surprising that Microsoft let Zune fade away as a stand-alone product by inserting it in its smartphone operating system: The Windows Phone operating system launched in 2011.

Both of these Microsoft entries (Zune and Windows Phone) were strong products and received high praise from many customers and industry followers. A classmate of mine from Stanford, Albert Shum, who had led the development of the Windows Phone operating system, sent me a demo phone to try out. My assessment was that Shum and his team had created a beautiful, thoughtful interface that could be a contender. But even with such a promising product that created a standout user experience from all angles, Microsoft is still having trouble making a dent in either the portable music player or mobile smartphone markets. What's the problem?

I say that Microsoft lacks the charisma it needs to get over the hurdle of being late to these markets. After nearly 40 years of demonstrating to the world a lack of coolness, a company like Microsoft can't easily convince the world that it is suddenly very sexy. Lack of charisma is just as powerful a momentum as having charisma to spare. Even technically excellent products won't be able to counteract a charisma deficit.

The charisma problem became the background to what has been an ongoing battle between Apple and Microsoft over the past decades—that is, and the battle between the charismatic Steve Jobs and the less-than-charismatic Bill Gates. The almost comical fight has been played out in nasty comments on both sides and in ads, such as Apple's "Mac versus PC" campaign, which perfectly captured the cool versus uncool aura surrounding each company. Jobs perhaps summarized his opinion most clearly when he pointed out in the 1996 documentary film *Triumph of the Nerds*, that "[Microsoft] has absolutely no taste. And I don't mean that in a small way, I mean that in a big way, in the sense that they don't think of original ideas, and they don't bring much culture into their products."[4] In his own polarizing way, what Jobs was really talking about was charisma.

Apple's Fifth Avenue Store in New York City is as carefully designed and executed as any Apple product. *Image: Apple Inc.*

34

Some companies and brands (and people) have a natural charisma, a built-in charm that is part of their DNA. But more often than not, it takes time and resources, smarts, and determined leadership to build and sustain the kind of charisma that Apple has. A commitment to design over such a long period of time has created a cocoon of charisma around Apple that sticks. Discipline and focus add to that image. You detect that confidence and cool and aura of invincibility every time you see or place an Apple product in your hand.

Remember that Apple is one of the most valuable companies in the world, even though it sells only a handful of products. As Tim Cook, Apple's CEO who took over after Jobs's death in 2011, pointed out at a Goldman Sachs technology conference in 2010, "We can put all our products on the table you're sitting at. Those products together sell $40 billion per year. No other company can make that claim except perhaps an oil company. We are the most focused company that I know of, or have read of, or have any knowledge of. We say no to good ideas every day; we say no to great ideas, to keep the number of things we focus on small in number."[5]

Step into an Apple Store anywhere in the world and you will understand how this intense focus plays out when the product meets the customer. The store is not merely a place to sell you a computer or an iPod. You can buy those things online or at other retailers. The Apple Store is the beautiful embodiment of the Apple brand and a wonderland where consumers can experience products, get help, and even attend classes and other events in an open, airy, and beautifully designed space. Apple recognizes that the future of retail resides is leveraging three things—place, people, and product—in a way that cannot be replicated by competitors or even by its own online store.

The Genius Bar in every store is just that, pure genius. Customers are lured to the store for free assistance with their Apple stuff, and in the process they are exposed to all the wonderful new products, accessories, and services that Apple offers. Moreover, the geniuses behind the Genius Bar have one-to-one access with their customers, thus creating the perfect sales situation for technology products that many customers find confusing. Who better to recommend the right (Apple) product than a "Genius," in one the softest sells in retail?

Apple Stores maximize the best things about a store and minimize the minutiae. Products (it's all about the products, after all) are laid out on white tables like objects in a museum that you can walk around and observe and, of course, touch to give you the hands-on experience. The youthful sales team is friendly and knowledgeable and never pushy. They are equipped with portable scanners to help complete the purchase and get you out the door. How about an e-mailed receipt? Absolutely! Apple wants to suck you into the store to buy the product and then get you home and using it with the utmost speed. That's part of the total experience that creates charisma.

> It's only a phone, of course, but with the charismatic impact of the company, the brand, the product, and the famous logo—not to mention Jobs himself—that phone became an instant star.

Apple used the same formula when it entered the portable music player market, in its own unique way, of course. Unlike the competition, Apple didn't focus only on the music player and its features and functions. As usual it looked at designing the entire experience of managing digital music, from downloading tunes to the device and then accessing these tunes on the go. What's more, because your Apple computer would be the hub of the system, the company shifted some of the usability load to the PC where the big screen, keyboard, and mouse helped ease some of the usual pain points along the way. The iPod software was minimized to focus on music playback, while iTunes on the computer was the central manager and the place where customers could buy their music. A Windows version of iTunes and the iTunes store followed.

With all the pieces of the experience in place, Apple was able to capitalize on the ecosystem it had created, which was founded on the initial observation that digital music could be better. And it was better; after all, you could get "1,000 songs in your pocket," as the Apple ad so rightly promised, summing up the iPod experience with a simple, insightful, and charismatic slogan.

Then there's the secrecy. Secrecy creates a mystique around the company and the products, especially when new ones are introduced. Apple, in fact, is the ultimate secret corporate machine, rivaled only by spy agencies and Willy Wonka's chocolate factory. Little if any information leaks out of Apple headquarters in Cupertino, and employees are sworn to a *Sopranos*-like cult of secrecy. With so few products and such a high premium on people (from customers to financial analysts) wanting to know what Apple will do next, Apple goes to extreme measures to protect information about product planning and development initiatives.

A former Apple engineer told me that engineers are given access to only the part of a product that they are working on. Only a handful of people see the whole product. Apple Global Security personnel deliver new products to stores in locked cases. One person at Apple, who was of course sworn to secrecy and couldn't reveal his name, summed up the company's core values for me this way: "Secrecy, teamwork, quality." Secrecy is a primary value that adds to Apple's charisma account.

That's especially important to build anticipation for product launches. To Apple's legions of fans and devotees—as well as stock market watchers—life revolves around the constant buzz and speculation about the company's next moves. When a product does make its debut, Apple goes all out to maximize the excitement. Steve Jobs, always the showboater, was a master at orchestrating these shows and milking the crowd for acclaim. Dressed in his Apple outfit of blue jeans and an Issey Miyake black turtleneck, he knew how to work the crowd and get them off their feet to see the latest Apple product. It's only a phone, of course, but with the charismatic impact of the company, the brand, the product, and the famous logo—not to mention Jobs himself—that phone became an instant star.

SUMMARY

Design can make all the difference to your company at the top and bottom lines if you embrace and leverage the power of design to create extreme emotional engagement. To achieve this, beauty, ingenuity, and charisma must become part of every product, service, and customer touch point. Once this is achieved, your products and services will stand out in even the most crowded field.

THE BUILDING BLOCKS

Beauty creates a remarkable and unmistakable first and lasting impression through the qualities of aesthetic attraction. Apple does this by focusing on principles such as thinness; the tactile feel of the product; and the all-important simplicity, with a focus on forms that are geometric and symmetric.

Ingenuity is a path that leads to emotional technology. New technology must always be human-centered, approachable, and natural for people to understand and use. Technology can surprise and delight customers, but the siren song of technology (robots anyone?) can lead us astray and away from immediate desires (more tablets, please).

Charisma will be the result if you pay close attention to the relationship you are creating with your customers through every touch point. A product with charisma has a certain mystique and charm, and a bit of secrecy about the company adds to that allure and builds expectations. A charismatic product makes the customer feel like the center of the universe.

DESIGN LIKE APPLE AGENDA

Before moving on to the second principle in Chapter 2, take a moment to answers these questions about your own projects and the products of your company:

1 How do your products and services rate on a scale of 1 to 10 when it comes to emotional engagement? A 10 on all dimensions gets you to beauty, ingenuity, and charisma. Be explicit about where you are strong and where you can improve.

2 Does your organization know what beauty means for your brand and customers? Are you aligned around a clear expression, like Apple's commitment to simplicity?

3 Are your company's products ingenious, or do they misalign technology with the customer needs? What is their intent? How do they rate on the charisma scale?

4 Where are the weak points in the product, services, advertising, retail, and support?

5 Is design considered essential within your organization, or is it window dressing? If you are a designer, accumulate the stories and evidence of how design makes a difference, and bring them to your organization in the context of how they can help create value.

Now let's turn our attention to designing an agile organization that will be the framework for the value that design can create.

Design the Organization

Nurture taste, talent, and a design culture.

You might not know about a company in Silicon Valley called SanDisk. It's not up there in the pantheon of technology and service companies that most people recognize along with Apple and Microsoft (or Facebook, Google, and Yahoo, for that matter). But SanDisk is a Fortune 500 multinational that is the world's largest dedicated provider of flash memory storage solutions.

In earlier days, flash memory was used to store the pictures you'd taken in your digital camera and the phone numbers of your friends in your cell phone. With the rise of computer networks and the subsequent demise of the floppy disk in the late 1990s, people still occasionally needed a way to conveniently store a few files in a format that would be easy to move from computer to computer without the hassle of connecting to a network. The USB connector had become a staple on computers and other devices, so by bolting flash memory onto a USB connector, companies began making thumb drives.

Founded in 1988, SanDisk was the leader in flash memory in the form of chips that were built directly into cameras and cell phones and also individual "cards" that you could plug into your digital camera, PDA, or mobile phone. When SanDisk decided it was time to make its own thumb drive, the company asked

LUNAR to help with the design. Why did a company that had been making flash memory for years, a leader in the field, need our help? This would be SanDisk's first three-dimensional product that went beyond its flat card memory products. The company didn't have designers in-house, and the decision makers thought that as long as they were moving in a new direction they might as well use design to make a statement and a good impression with customers and the market.

Rather than create a thumb drive with fixed memory hidden inside, SanDisk reckoned it would be better to equip its thumb drive with a removable secure digital (SD) card, which was a popular format at the time. With that mandate, we designed and engineered a product called the Cruzer, which was as much a thumb drive as it was a go-between to get your pictures off the camera and onto the computer. Cruzer resembled a turtle: In its stored position, the head and limbs were all tucked inside a protective shell, but by sliding the switch on the top of the device you could expose the USB "head." Slide it in the opposite direction and the SD card, or "tail," popped out. Shifting to neutral secured the connector and card inside the shell, as if the turtle were in the tucked-in defensive mode.

For several years, SanDisk retained us to help design a range of thumb drives, adapters, and even portable digital music players, and we worked hard to bring a level of beauty and ingenuity to this new family of products so they would rise above the ordinary and the mundane and have a touch of charisma. But these efforts were threatened by companies known as original equipment manufacturers (OEMs), which pitch new products to companies that come already designed and tooled and ready to have a name and a label—*any label*—slapped on.

OEMs allow companies like SanDisk to buy, package, and drop new products into their established retail distribution network.

The SanDisk Cruzer was a uniquely-designed portable USB flash drive that featured removable media in a package that protected the USB connector without the need for a cap. *Image: Sandbox Studio*

These products don't have the heart, soul, and design savvy of the products we were designing for SanDisk, but they are enticing for any company. Companies like SanDisk are constantly bombarded by offers from OEMs, and how can they refuse such a great offer? How does a product manager or a chief executive say no to a plug-and-play revenue stream? You don't have to hire a design firm or worry about prototyping, development, and production. No fuss, no mess, and the product is in the pipeline to customers in the blink of an eye.

When a company adds products to its catalog in this way, it risks sending a message to customers that the brand is just a middleman that resells random products from other manufacturers. It demonstrates that there is at most a soft commitment to using design as a compelling differentiator. This can easily happen when there is no guiding design voice or the presence of a design tastemaker in the organization.

In Chapter 1, I discussed how Apple drives design to the extreme emotional engagement of beauty, ingenuity, and charisma to generate blockbuster products. But for most companies, there are always temptations to take shortcuts or to be distracted by short-term opportunities (e.g., the OEMs flirting with SanDisk and offering fast solutions to product design and revenue growth). How can a company—especially a public one, like SanDisk, that is responsible to its shareholders—resist such temptations and the promise of increased market share?

The secret is to establish core design values in your organization that are nonnegotiable priorities and embed them in the corporate culture. To achieve this, you must acquire design taste, hire the right design talent, and then weave these design values and culture into the fabric of the organization. In addition, there must be a person who functions as the arbiter of taste and who maintains the design standards and values.

TASTE

The life trajectories of two of the most influential men of the high-tech era, Steve Jobs and his longtime rival at Microsoft, Bill Gates, are uncannily similar. Both were born in 1955; both became technology wizards in high school and later were college dropouts. They each founded and built companies whose products and services have changed the way we live and work and interact with computers. But that's where the similarities end and the design divergence begins.

Gates was a master software entrepreneur who through partnerships and licensing deals dominated the personal computer market and gobbled up market share in that domain. Gaining market share was his driving passion, while design rarely figured into his business plan. By extreme contrast, of course, Jobs formed Apple around the concept of design and saw everything through that lens. Apple has a deep and abiding sense of *design taste*. Microsoft does not.

A remarkably funny video that went viral in 2006 brought into sharp focus Microsoft's lack of commitment to design. Accompanied by the driving assembly-line rhythm of Danny Elfman's "Breakfast Machine," the video imagines what the design process at Microsoft would have been like if that company had created packaging for Apple's iPod. The Microsoft team starts with Apple's sleekly minimalist white box from 2005 and reworks it to meet the less rigorous standards of typical Microsoft packaging. The video, with the tongue-in-cheek title "Microsoft Redesigns iPod Packaging," shows the austere iPod box being overloaded with words, charts, logos, hard-to-read regulations, and an assortment of flags and banners. Quotes periodically show up on screen in the voice of the well-meaning marketing manager who is directing the design team's work on the box. The box becomes a cheap, overworked mess, indistinguishable

Snippets from a video that was leaked onto the Internet parodying the Microsoft approach to package design by asking what if it had created the iPod package. It's hard for most organizations to deliver the kind of impactful simplicity that Apple employs.

44

"Make sure you're on brand."

Microsoft designs the iPod package.™

re- *2005*
Microsoft®

"I'd say that's got some shelf presence."

from any other product on a store shelf. "It really stands out!" the final caption proudly proclaims.[1]

The video is both funny and revealing, as it bluntly portrays the Microsoft way of thinking—so much so that you'd think Apple had concocted this unflattering portrait to mock its rival. Yet it was actually made internally by Microsoft's packaging designers to challenge the marketing team to do better. Much to its credit, Microsoft itself recognized the need to ratchet up its design bona fides.

Design taste is always tough to define. One day, while standing in a drugstore checkout line, I found myself staring at an ugly clock. It was hanging on a wall at the front of the store for all to see. It wasn't a regular sort of ugly; it was horribly ugly. Call it nuclear ugly. Sliced from some unsuspecting tree trunk that never hurt anybody, the heavily shellacked face of the clock preserved pictures of red roses and drippy script type that spelled "LOVE." The hands and numbers were plastic, with a cheap layer of shiny gold crap covering them.

I was just buying some razor blades, but here I was, my disdain for this object growing in intensity. Then, out of the blue, the woman in front of me pointed at the monstrosity of a clock. "Honey," she said to the young girl accompanying her. "Go see how much that is." My own mother is known for a number of sayings that I carry around with me and like to quote when the moment is right. One of them perfectly fit this moment: "There's no accounting for taste."

That also applies to design. Before the first iPhone was launched in 2007, a client of ours was using a focus group to get feedback on preferences and habits related to certain electronic products. "They should all be black and silver," declared a rather vocal leader in the group. Everyone else nodded in submission.

"Yes, black and silver," they droned in unison. Then the moderator checked the time on her Motorola Cobalt phone, a lustrous blue, folding number with silver trim. Everyone ogled the phone. Then they changed their votes to multicolored products.

Many manufacturers fear that after the long, hard slog of developing a new product and getting it out the door, the market will reject it because of its looks. More often than not, this happens because the managers listen too intently to focus groups. So many products are made without clear attention to the concept of beauty or because they simply borrow their aesthetic from other successful products. The fear of offending customers outweighs the trust in taste.

> "You can't just ask customers what they want and then try to give that to them. By the time you get it built, they'll want something new."

Apple takes a radically different approach to taste. Jobs distrusted focus groups and instead looked inside Apple—to his designers and other people throughout the organization—for direction on what products to make, which features to include, and how a product should look. Instead of following the herd, he wanted Apple to lead the way, to be the industry tastemaker. "You can't just ask customers what they want and then try to give that to them. By the time you get it built, they'll want something new,"[2] he told *Inc.* magazine in April 1989 when he was awarded the publication's Entrepreneur of the Decade Award. Jobs never let go of that belief. In 1998 he told *BusinessWeek*, "It's really hard to design products by focus groups. A lot of times, people don't know what they want until you show it to them."[3]

Taste is by definition idiosyncratic and very personal. To have taste means that there will always be someone with a different taste who doesn't like your taste. There really is no accounting for taste (Mom, you were right on this one) and no absolute measure for it. Some organizations rely on data to create taste, but that can end up with products as bland and generic as Muzak, the elevator music we hear everywhere. Muzak isn't really music but background ambiance for public spaces that is programmed not to offend anyone. I think of it as the opposite of music. Music is created from an individual voice. It's the voice and taste of the artist, and we are free to like it or not.

Like a great musician, Apple creates a unique voice and expresses its taste so confidently that the company became a tastemaker, a leader that others follow. Not everybody liked the iPhone when it was launched in 2007, but by 2012 nearly every smartphone maker on the planet was following its lead and formula and selling a device that looked like an iPhone. The were all making phones that looked like a glossy, black and metal slab with rounded corners.

The glossy, black and metal slab came about because Jobs had acquired great design taste, even though he wasn't really a designer. Or was he? That depends on the definition we use. Jobs wasn't a designer, because he didn't have a degree in any design field. In his professional life, he didn't directly engage in the kind of creative work that we usually associate with professional designers.

Yet you needn't have designer credentials to think and act as a designer. Jobs exemplified many of the traits of a great designer: He was creative, curious, exploratory, and playful. His father had taught him that it was important to care about the craft of anything you built. Influenced by Zen philosophy, Jobs paid close attention to the world around him and came to appreciate the kind of simple, refined aesthetic we often associate with Japan.

Jobs also had a number of formative interactions with design that he clung to with the obsessive passion that was central to his personality. In his commencement address to Stanford University

Apple created the glossy, black and metal slab icon that became the archetype for most smartphones. *Images: iStockphoto*

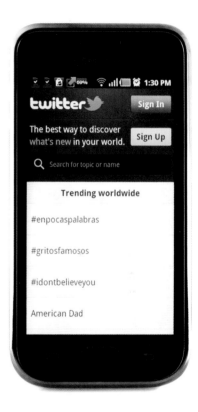

in 2005, Jobs spoke about a calligraphy class he had taken many years ago. "I learned about serif and sans-serif typefaces, about varying the space between different letter combinations, about what makes great typography great. It was beautiful.... [W]hen we were designing the first Macintosh computer, it all came back to me. And we designed it all into the Mac. It was the first computer with beautiful typography. If I had never dropped in on that single course in college, the Mac would never have multiple typefaces or proportionally spaced fonts."[4]

We could say that Jobs was most definitely a designer because he appreciated beautiful objects and was determined to make Apple products beautiful, too. He was insatiable in his search for new ideas, materials, and technology. He had developed design taste.

I use the word *taste* on purpose, to be provocative. Design is about being intentional at every point. Without taste and without intention, you can sell products that make money but do not represent the company's core values. Committing to a sense of taste means that you create your own charismatic products, or you create a process that enables your OEMs to show up with new products that reflect your own design taste. That intent begins at the top; at Apple it was Jobs and Senior Vice President of Design Jonathan (Jony) Ive who were the curators of Apple design and the Apple brand. They controlled the design and development process from the top down, and they made the final call on every product that bears the Apple name. They were the curators and arbiters of Apple's design taste.

That's not the only model, however, to create a singular vision of taste at a company. If there's no Steve Jobs or Jony Ive running the show and setting the standard at your company, you can articulate a set of design tenets or a design philosophy to help the organization understand the vision. Working together as a team with this vision in mind can lead to beautiful, intentional products that are as appealing to customers as those that come out of the Apple shop.

The danger is that without these definitions and commitments, a company's products might end up being curated by disparate voices within the organization. This is like staging an art exhibition with a dozen curators in charge, all of them bringing their own individual vision to the show. This robs the exhibition of a strong singular vision and intent, just as a company's products would lack a unified design vision that confuses the customer. One company that has developed a coherent design philosophy is Herman Miller, the U.S. furniture manufacturer. This company has established 10 tenets of design—including design that is "human-centered," "purposeful," and "spirited"—to encapsulate a way of thinking about design. These tenets find their way into the design of each product.

As the leader of a company, it is imperative for you to recognize the role you can play as an arbiter of taste. I have met many executives who believe this and have become the chief curators at their company. They articulate a design philosophy that outlines threshold requirements for products and defines their intent, as well as delineating what products should *not* be. A Ferrari will not have cup holders.

You might be thinking that the role of design guru isn't for you, that you're not that kind of person, that wasting time worrying about taste and beauty is not the best use of your valuable time. It can be tough to let go of these assumptions and to let yourself become a tastemaker like Steve Jobs, or to delegate that task to others. Either way, to design like Apple, it is essential to take design taste and curation seriously, because it helps a company better understand its products and where to take them, as well as its customers and what will make them happy.

TALENT

Given his blustery and compulsive personality, we can imagine Jobs as a design tyrant who imposed his will on everyone at Apple. But it wasn't that simple. Jobs also hired and cultivated a great number of people that he respected and trusted to be part of his "insanely great" team. He pursued and assembled *design talent* that helped him implement Apple's design philosophy.

One of those creative people was Hartmut Esslinger, head of the design firm Frog, which Jobs tapped as Apple's design agency of record in 1983. Frog, based in Germany, then opened an office in Silicon Valley, which was a bold move in the consulting world to support just one client. Jobs and Esslinger clicked. Jobs especially liked dealing directly with the head of a respected design firm as they worked together on perfecting Apple products and creating a unified design vision, beginning with the Macintosh SE.

> Jobs promoted Ive to senior vice president, an acknowledgment of the central role Jobs ascribed to design.

When Jobs returned to Apple in 1997, he connected with Ive, the chief industrial designer who had been hired when Jobs was not at the company. Together they became Apple's tastemakers. Jobs promoted Ive to senior vice president, an acknowledgment of the central role Jobs ascribed to design. Within Apple the unusually tight bond between Jobs and Ive became crucial to spreading the company's design mantra and ethos throughout the organization.

Luckily both men shared an admiration for a concept of design that had originated in the German Bauhaus movement of the 1930s, which espoused a modernist view that eschews ornamentation and emphasizes function over everything else.

Jobs created a strong, direct relationship with Frog founder, Esslinger, to establish the design language for Apple that led to products like the Macintosh SE. *Image: Danamania, Wikipedia*

Jobs and Ive also trusted each other. They ate lunch together "almost every day when Jobs was healthy and in the office," Walter Isaacson writes in his biography of Steve Jobs.[5] Jobs kept close tabs on the design team and what they were doing. He often spent time in the studio observing team members and speaking with them about projects and problems. He didn't read about what the designers were doing in e-mail; he saw what was on their desks and heard what was on their minds, and he didn't refrain from commenting on what they were doing, or cajoling— some might say bullying—them to do better.

You can build this design capability internally, as Jobs did with Ive and his team. Or it can be done externally, in a relationship with an outside design firm such as Frog, with its strong leader Esslinger. At my firm, we pursue this type of design consulting relationship with a variety of companies. From my experience, they work best when a very senior person inside the company is in a position of authority to make a consistent commitment to design over a sustained period of time.

At Herman Miller, the design team is relatively small, given the company's outsized commitment to design and its reputation as a design leader in the furniture industry. Gary Smith, director of Design Facilitation at Herman Miller, is in charge of leveraging talented designers outside of the company. "My title describes my role exactly," he explained to me. "I am not a manager so much as a facilitator, finding designers outside of our walls to create excellent, original designs for Herman Miller that also respect and reflect the historical importance of design to our brand and culture." Herman Miller's approach to design is different than Apple's, but nonetheless very successful. Apple creates products with an identical voice; Herman Miller's products represent a range of design voices, and the company ensures that all of these products live up to the company's design ideals. You could almost think of

Herman Miller lives by 10 tenets of design
that ensure their products embrace the same
philosophy while not necessarily looking
the same. *Images: Courtesy Herman Miller, Inc.*

Herman Miller as a record label that brings in a variety of the most creative musicians—in, say, jazz or pop or classical—where each one makes different music, yet all have the same discerning sense of taste. Both the Apple and Herman Miller approaches to inculcating design taste can work for your company.

CULTURE

In 2011, a supplier to the automotive industry approached us. For confidentiality reasons, I can't reveal all the details about this client, but it was clear that this company had a problem. While it was only a component supplier, it seemed that its customers—the carmakers—were disappointed with the company's commitment to design. In fact a sports car manufacturer, which had been to its office to evaluate the company's suitability as a partner in developing technology components for an upcoming platform, came away being less than impressed with its design chops.

This particular supplier had been successful for many years based solely on its technical capabilities. It had a very small design team, because it was in the habit of letting the carmakers do their own design around the components that this particular company produced. But as technology increasingly finds its way to cars—from GPS to entertainment and night vision systems— carmakers are learning from consumer-electronics companies like Apple and looking to their suppliers to develop a design point of view. They want every company that is involved in creating the car, including parts suppliers, to be thinking about the customer and how design can speak to the driver behind the wheel.

This supplier didn't want us to design a chic digital speedometer. It needed us to figure out how to put together a design team that would help it compete and win over clients, the carmakers. All of a sudden, design had become the company's most critical need. The senior engineering manager who called us knew that the problem would not be fixed just by adding designers to its research and development centers around the world. This company needed to change the way it thought about design and what design could bring to the company. To reap the rewards of design, it would have to create a *design culture.*

Over the past 20 years or so (call it the age of Apple) design has definitely made advances as an important component in the development of products and services. But it's still primarily used as window dressing to create a pretty package rather than as an approach that determines the entire creative culture of a company. Many of our clients seek our help only when they have a special need for innovation. They've been able to free up some cash to pursue an innovation effort, a project that is usually outside the realm of their conventional development programs. That has little to do with creating a culture of design. Design must become part of your company's DNA if you are going to design like Apple and achieve the advantages of beauty, ingenuity, and charisma that I discussed in Chapter 1.

> "Design isn't any one team. There are people taking risks all over the company."

To do this, teams at every level in an organization must learn to think like designers. By that I mean they explore options, question the status quo, and take risks, whether they are in the design studio or the marketing or packaging department. At Apple, it was Ive, the design director, who usually got all the credit. But Tony Fadell pointed out to me in an interview that at Apple, "Design isn't any one team. There are people taking risks all over the company." Design is a way of thinking and acting that permeates Apple because the company has instilled a design culture.

That design culture is often reflected in Apple ads. The now iconic "Think Different" campaign from the late 1990s, created by its long-standing ad agency Chiat\Day, featured notables such as Albert Einstein, Bob Dylan, Martin Luther King Jr., and Gandhi, who were presented as mischievous, upstart, outsider personalities. "Here's to the crazy ones," the copy began. "The misfits. The rebels. The troublemakers." No computers are seen in the ads. Nor are they needed. Those misfits, rebels, and troublemakers referred, of course, to Apple itself and to its technology and the culture of design (with its upstart, outsider, and mischievous tendencies) that Jobs had created and that sets Apple apart from other companies, especially its archrival Microsoft.

No history of Apple and its design culture is complete without acknowledging the pioneering work of Bob McKim, a former professor of design and engineering at Stanford University. McKim influenced many of the creative people who gravitated to Apple and other companies because he brought together the seemingly disparate worlds of design and engineering with a course of study in the 1960s called Product Design. The earliest designers at Apple, including Jerry Manock and Bill Dresselhaus, who between them designed the Apple II, the Apple III, the Lisa, and the Macintosh, were graduates of this program.

McKim drew on both the arts and sciences and encouraged students to move between the two. He saw a direct link between a person's ability to draw, imagine, and see and believed that your interests and skills shape your perceptions of the world around you. McKim put his ideas together in a course that is still taught today. Called Visual Thinking, it teaches Stanford engineering students right-brain skills like sketching, prototyping, and lateral thinking approaches to problem solving.[6]

I have taught this course several times at Stanford and always marvel at the reaction these future engineers, with their penchant for sober analytical thinking, have toward the class. "I felt like I was in kindergarten again," is not an uncommon refrain. For many students, the reason they feel like they're in kindergarten is because they haven't used that part of their brain for 15 years. I see a similar thing taking place at Apple: There is a mash-up of great technology and operational excellence with chaotic and experimental exploration.

Stop for a moment and think about your own experience. If you are a manager you, might be wincing while reading this book, waiting for the mathematical proof or the market statistics that demonstrate how design will predictably revolutionize your business. Where is the process or the playbook, you might be wondering, to accomplish these goals? Because you are analytical, future-oriented, and conscious of productivity, you are questioning what you will learn to sharpen your skill and competitiveness and improve the bottom line. You might be scratching your head and puzzling over why you should even care about design.

But let's say you are a graphic designer. After glancing at only a few pages, you will have instantly noticed many details about this book, like the justified text layout on this page, the paper stock, the serif typeface, and the tabs along the right-hand edge. You could close the book now and recall all of those features in detail. As a designer, you are more comfortable in the moment and aware of visual relationships and how the pieces fit together for their intended use. Designers see things in the world in detail because they spend time creating their own things. They can imagine things that don't yet exist, because they have experience in seeing and creating.

What about your own creative abilities? Do you marvel at the way some people can regularly come up with out-of-the-box ideas that no one else in the room thinks of? In my experience, more people in the world can write a detailed marketing-requirements document or understand a financial statement than can stand at a whiteboard and make an understandable sketch of a product they are imagining.

Apple focuses on hiring people who "get" the Apple culture, according to Larry Tesler, the legendary software designer and early pioneer of the graphical user interface (GUI) at Xerox Parc and at Apple. In other words, Apple likes to hire people who hew to McKim's view of the world. Invariably, these people have something going for them in the arts, Tesler recalls. They might be fine artists or musicians outside of their usual gigs as engineers and software geeks. Says Tesler, "The big insight in those days was that great people created a great process. It's not the process that makes the people great." That became the foundation of the Apple design culture.

Yet it's not enough to simply hire people with great creative talent and slip them into an existing organization. As we saw in the Motorola story in Chapter 1 and with the automotive component supplier in this chapter, if design is isolated in a department and doesn't filter across the entire organization, it's easy to dampen or even kill its impact.

Think of design as a kind of beneficial virus inside a corporation. It's small, but it can spread wildly and wield considerable influence. Because of that, it also has a great many enemies. Most corporations are filled with people who, for whatever reason (usually self-preservation and fear of the new), see themselves as the antibodies to the design virus and try to inhibit progress. They strive to preserve the organization as it is. They might appear to roam the hallways and meeting rooms in search of new ideas, but then they kill them on contact with extraordinary skill.

> If design is isolated in a department and doesn't filter across the entire organization, it's easy to dampen or even kill its impact.

That's too bad, because in my experience there's no shortage of ideas out there. When people hear about what I do, they are all eager to tell me about some idea they have. The real trick is not in finding the great idea but in knowing how to execute the right idea, which is the goal of a creative culture. At the memorial for Steve Jobs held by Apple for its employees around the world, Ive gave a moving tribute to Jobs's role in protecting ideas. "[J]ust as Steve loved ideas, and loved making stuff, he treated the process of creativity with a rare and a wonderful reverence. You see, I think he, better than anyone, understood that while ideas ultimately can be so powerful, they begin as fragile, barely formed thoughts, so easily missed, so easily compromised, so easily just squished."

Looking back on the Jobs era, I see him as someone who put Apple in a unique position. As the founder and leader (and even with a break in his tenure), Jobs had the chance to bake design into the vision of the company, and the design culture grew out of that vision. He drove the company to be creative and to innovate continuously, as if it were always an enterprising, high-energy start-up. "Apple is the biggest startup in the world,"[7] Jobs told Walter Mossberg, the *Wall Street Journal*'s technology correspondent in 2010 at the D conference. With Jobs at the helm, Apple never veered from the top-down design management approach of its visionary founder.

To be sure, it helped that Jobs was the founder. Founders have the opportunity and the will to shape the kind of company they want, whereas nonfounding managers usually don't. Founders are clear about what they want to do, and they can transmit that to their staff. The whole company works hard together in a creative, flexible, and oftentimes chaotic environment to get the enterprise off the ground. Fadell summarized the difference for me: "Founders treat their companies like their own kids, and they are more comfortable taking risks with them. You're not going to take someone else's kids bungee jumping."

If you are a founder, consider yourself lucky. You can influence the culture you would like your company to follow and embrace. You can follow in the footsteps of Jobs and his strict culture of design by hiring engineers with liberal arts leanings. Or you can emulate Jeff Bezos of Amazon, where risk taking is encouraged. Or make a commitment to customer service like Tony Hsieh of online shoes and clothing retailer Zappos.

At some point, however, successful companies must move beyond their founders. That's where Apple finds itself today, following the death of Jobs in 2011. I once thought Apple wouldn't survive without Jobs, because he was just too important to the entire culture he had created. But in researching material for this book I've come to realize that Jobs instilled several key attributes in his company, as outlined in Jim Collins's successful business book *Built to Last*, that are necessary for survival after the founder departs.

One of them is a cultlike culture, in which employees believe they are part of an elite team that shares an ideology not found at other companies. Another idea that Apple embodies is what Collins calls the Big Hairy Audacious Goal: a belief among the faithful that they are making a difference with their products, which are inherently better than those made by other companies.

Many people already work in a company with an established culture and a well-defined and ingrained approach to doing things. That culture probably doesn't focus on design. But have no fear. You can make a difference with design even in a company with an established culture like our old punching bag, Microsoft.

Although we make fun of Microsoft for its apparent lack of design awareness, nobody can dispute the fact that the company is a market success and a credit to Bill Gates as a business visionary. Many talented people in its ranks have helped create the ubiquitous software that billions of people use every day. True, Microsoft hasn't created many products that meet the standards of beauty, ingenuity, and charisma that I have outlined. But I would be dishonest not to acknowledge many bright spots in the company's product history that deserve a closer look, especially now, when I believe Microsoft is changing its attitude about design and allowing a new design culture to take root.

"Design too often describes the final thing that you make, instead of the way you get there."

Microsoft's Albert Shum explained it to me this way. "All the technology in the world doesn't mean that you're going to make a great product. It's about getting the right balance of the rational and the emotional." That sounds exactly like something Steve Jobs would have said about the coming together of science and the liberal arts and the need for products to connect on a deeper level with customers.

Shum also points out the hurdles facing Microsoft with its existing culture. There is an open culture at the company, which in many ways is a good thing. But the downside is that "everyone does their own thing," Shum explains. Such freedom can lead to products that are unfocused and don't reflect a unified design voice (unlike at Apple, where everyone is on the same page about design culture). Freedom means there is no overriding design ethos or philosophy. Design is diffused. Every marketing manager has a say and pushes for something different, as Microsoft's satirical packaging video suggests.

Shum is trying to create a design ethos at Microsoft. In an echo of the Herman Miller approach, he is establishing an aspirational design playbook to help infect the organization with a design culture. The challenge is to get everyone on the Microsoft team, from the marketers and developers to the technologists, and to align them around a single vision. "Design too often describes the final thing that you make, instead of the way you get there," Shum says. He's talking about a design culture like Apple, of course, which he acknowledges as a model. "We strive to make products where every last detail was considered, intentional. Isn't that what we like so much about Apple products?"

Shum rallies individuals involved with his projects from across the company by developing a narrative and then bringing others along. With the end customer in mind, he is always asking, "What is the story that we're building for the customer?" His view is that customers don't look at the range of products and their brand and messaging as different elements of a company. Customers see all of these as components as part of a single story. "You have to get people believing in what you're doing," Shum explains. "That's why I'm moving into a role that encompasses not only product but brand, too."

Microsoft's Zune music player and Windows Phone suggest that the company is capable of delivering great products and that Shum's efforts to overhaul the design culture could lead to more. What we can learn from this story about Microsoft is that there are consequences for a lack of design culture. And any company or organization can change and integrate design taste, talent, and culture into its DNA so that a structure and framework exists to create great products and services.

The simple and engaging Windows Phone operating system running on a Nokia Lumia handset that stands out for its clear reinterpretation of the smartphone slab.
Image: Nokia

SUMMARY

To design like Apple means creating an organization around the concepts of design taste, talent, and culture. You must have an arbiter of taste, an empowered team of designers, and widespread behaviors throughout the company that reward creative thinking, risk taking, and experimentation. To design like Apple is to establish and nurture a set of strong, nonnegotiable design values that create the extreme emotional engagement of beauty, ingenuity, and charisma throughout the company.

THE BUILDING BLOCKS

Design taste can be acquired through education or personal background and interests and is enhanced by surrounding yourself with creative people. An organization that is designed like Apple will have a tastemaker near the top of the organization to curate the design outcomes of the company, and this person will have an established design philosophy or vision.

Design talent refers to a dedicated design capability, whether an internal team of designers or retained external designers and design firms that bring the design vision to life and carry out development of products and services.

Design culture results when an organization's leaders value design and hire people who have a diverse appreciation of creativity, regardless of job responsibilities. Design culture is a beneficial virus that spreads wildly and influences all aspects of an organization. Design culture can be baked into the company by a founder or added later, when a company decides that design values will be beneficial.

DESIGN LIKE APPLE AGENDA

Before moving on to the focus on products in Chapter 3, consider the readiness of your team to create insanely great products by answering the following questions:

1 Even if you're not a designer by training, do you have design taste? If you don't have the time and inclination to do so, should

you create a senior design role at your company to curate the output of the entire organization from a design point of view? Jobs and Ive have been the arbiters of taste at Apple; Smith facilitates good design at Herman Miller; and Shum is changing the design culture at Microsoft.

2 Do your products exude a confidence, intentionality, and consistency rooted in a clearly articulated design playbook? Do your products adhere to a unified design vision or philosophy that is spelled out as an actionable design philosophy for staff to keep in mind at all times? Follow Herman Miller's example and create your own tenets of design.

3 Most modern companies have an awareness that design is important to the products and services they make. What's the state of that awareness at your company based on the scale, "Design is added on at the end of product development" at the low end to "We support design creativity at all levels and in everyone's job" at the opposite end?

4 One metric for the design values of an organization is that everyone knows which behaviors are discouraged. Would cutting corners on a design be considered acceptable?

5 Finding the right design talent is essential to promoting design in your company. To design like Apple, you need creative people who can bridge liberal arts and technology. Do you seek people with diverse creative interests, even for positions that don't directly require creativity thinking?

The Product Is the Marketing

Great products sell themselves.

Back in 1972, brand recognition was all you needed to sell a product. Major companies like consumer-goods manufacturers could easily correlate their advertising and television media buying budgets with sales figures. For a laundry detergent manufacturer, the performance of the detergent and its chemical formulation were less important than the brand name that a customer recognized. Procter & Gamble, for example, introduced Tide laundry detergent in 1946, backed by a $21 million ad campaign that made it the top selling brand in the country within two years, which continued well into the twenty-first century.

Technology has upended this strategy. Television advertising has declined with the arrival of VCRs, TiVo, YouTube, Hulu, OnDemand, Netflix, and whatever is coming next that lets the customer decide which ads to watch—or perhaps to blithely ignore your ads altogether. The Internet and social media are the new conduits for information, and that has led to a sea change in the way people perceive products and make judgments about them. In the 1970s, you might have been swayed by ads for a painkiller such as Excedrin (each type of headache had a specific number, such as "Excedrin headache number 10" for a "screaming child"), but today you hear a million voices on websites and through social media trumpeting the benefits or drawbacks of a particular brand.

The Internet, with its instant feedback and information overload, is the great leveler of our generation when it comes to a product's success or failure. Advertising and branding still play important roles, but advertising and branding can no longer make false claims about a product and get away with it for very long. The Internet speaks too loudly. And too quickly: Your product will be praised or pilloried in seconds.

In his 2003 book *Purple Cow*, Seth Godin reinforces this notion. He suggests that in the post–television advertising era, it's prudent to invest less in advertising and more in R&D if you want your product to stand out in a cluttered marketplace. These standouts are the so-called purple cows that you notice while driving by a field of ordinary black-and-white Holsteins. "Remarkable marketing is the art of building things worth noticing right into your product or service," Godin writes. "If your offering isn't remarkable, it is invisible."[1]

It's true. As customers, we are confronted every day with a mind-boggling array of products in stores and online, as well as the marketing and ad campaigns pushing us to buy one brand or another. How we sift through the clutter and noise and decide to choose one product or the other has kept psychologists, economists, and marketers busy for years as they seek the perfect strategy to attract our attention and harness our purchasing power. As a designer, my view is that the product is now the ultimate message, and to reinforce that message the product must be of exceptionally high quality and part of a pattern of repetition.

MESSAGE

Apple under Steve Jobs has always championed products. "What Jobs loved most was products,"[2] Adam Lashinsky writes in his book, *Inside Apple.* Products anchor the company and are the primary lens through which the customer perceives the brand.

Apple invests heavily in advertising, too, but the advertising is focused on the product (with the formidable exception of the 1997 "Think Different" campaign).

Apple spent $691 million on advertising in 2010, a big increase over the previous year due to the launch of the iPad and the iPhone 4. That seems like a remarkable amount of money, but it is actually just a small percentage of its annual revenue, which reached $108 billion in 2011. Yet even without spending a penny, Apple's brand would resonate just as loudly with customers. The reason is Apple's relentless commitment to the product. Marketing and advertising leverages that good work, not the other way around. All the money in the world spent on ads won't help a "just good enough" product become an insanely great one. As Amazon's chief executive put it at a shareholders meeting in 2009, "Advertising is the price you pay for having an unremarkable product or service." Create great products; then you can promote them.

The product is now the ultimate message, and to reinforce that message the product must be of exceptionally high quality and part of a pattern of repetition.

Author Scott Ginsberg is more colorful in his description of the pivotal role played designing a great product. "Marketing is like sex—if you have to pay for it, you're doing something wrong," he writes. "Smart companies spend money earlier in the process. Smart companies build things worth noticing right into the product ahead of time. Take design, for example. It's not an extra, it's not an also and it's not an accident—it's everything."[3] The temptation to favor empty messaging over great products is sill strong. To wit: a dancing elf.

The dancing elf, courtesy of on OfficeMax online media campaign called "Elf Yourself," appeared in 2007. It let you upload a picture of yourself to attach to an animated elf doing a hilarious dance. You then e-mailed it to friends who added their self-made dancing elves. And on it went from one person to another, a viral version of a chain letter zipping across the web. After wiping away tears of laughter, you realize that this type of new cheap trick—a self-distributing ad—is very effective. An advertiser saves ad dollars, and the message rides the wave of personal recommendation.

But for all the belly laughs it produced, this ad had a critical flaw. I couldn't remember which company was behind it. Was it Staples, OfficeMax, or Office Depot? The video was adorable, but it had nothing to do with buying office supplies or OfficeMax's value proposition. Yes, it generated views. But there was no connection to OfficeMax in the mind of a shopper wanting to buy pens and printer cartridges at a competitive price. People were talking about the dancing elf, not the great products, prices, and services available at OfficeMax.

The real question concerns OfficeMax's differentiation, or lack thereof. What is its remarkable product? How do we distinguish this office supplier from Staples and Office Depot? Ultimately, the company's clever viral campaign could not make up for the lack of a differentiated message. If you have remarkable, well-designed products that really connect with people, these products create their own following. They are amplified by advertising and marketing campaigns that help propel a message that you have already established with your unique offering.

Now think about the many products you have bought, cherished, and shared the most. How many of them had brilliant design? How many of the products at your own company have the same qualities? As a manager, the key questions you need to answer are these: Do your products stand on their own without additional marketing? Are you creating remarkable products that create a long-lasting consumer following? If you use this benchmark for judging how remarkable (or unremarkable) your products are, the design will be the best (or worst) advertisement of all.

The wide gap between great and merely good products can best be seen in toothbrushes. Yes, toothbrushes.

For a long time, toothbrushes were commodity products that were largely supported by network television advertising. With the declining influence of this type of messaging, manufacturers increasingly turned to design to create differentiation in what would become the ruthlessly competitive toothbrush market.

The toothbrush shelf in the grocery store exploded with apparent innovations that promised to clean teeth better. Flexible necks would put less pressure on your gums. Angled brushes provided an ergonomic advantage and more serious cleaning. Blue bristles that turned white were a reminder to replace a brush that had become less effective. Fighting for the toothbrush dollar, toothbrush makers spouted pseudoscience to claim that their brush was more effective because of a soft grip handle or special bristles or gum-massaging fingers.

One toothbrush from Reach was famous for claiming to be the most ergonomic brush on the market. It featured a bent neck that made it look like a tool your dentist would use. But on closer analysis, the design only borrowed a visual element from a professional dental tool rather than providing a true design benefit to sleepy consumers. In fact, the bend in the handle made sense only for the dentist; you would have to hold your hand as far back as your ear to brush your front teeth.

The design of the Reach toothbrush is flat-out wrong. At LUNAR, we discovered this fact when Oral-B, a rival toothbrush maker, hired us to create a new flagship design for its toothbrush family. To do this, Oral-B needed a breakthrough product. To achieve a breakthrough product, we needed to understand how people hold toothbrushes and all the minute details to do with toothbrushing. Otherwise, we wouldn't be to create a design that truly resonated with people as they performed this mundane daily task.

Surprisingly, Oral-B had little cataloged understanding (for a toothbrush manufacturer) about how people hold their toothbrushes. We recommended engaging an ergonomic design and research house, Metaphase, to help answer this fundamental question. Because time was of the essence, however, we initiated our own research and design work in parallel.

That work didn't involve following sleepy pajama-clad customers into their bathrooms. But we did conduct guerrilla research among our own staff and at any location where toothbrushes were sold. With the tenacity of archeologists digging amid ruins, we collected a wide range and variety of brushes and analyzed them according to their features and putative benefits. We began prototyping ideas right away by bending conventional toothbrushes into different shapes and trying them out ourselves. That's when we first noticed that the Reach toothbrush, although telegraphing better ergonomics with its bent form, was actually making us contort our wrists at strange angles to accommodate the otherwise simple task of brushing. Where's the ergonomic advantage in that?

Meanwhile, the researchers at Metaphase had reported from the field that people hold toothbrushes in some combination of five basic grips. Our designers trained themselves to use all five grips, and we continued prototyping. Working first with sketches before moving to foam models, we quickly tested for comfort and quality among the designers and engineers in our office. (There is more about the advantages and techniques of prototyping in Chapter 5.)

Before long, the designers came up with a "good enough" product. That's the moment when most companies pull the trigger and

The Oral-B CrossAction toothbrush leveraged better design to capture another five points of market share.
Image: LUNAR

rush the product to market. But Oral-B knew that every product requires a huge investment to start manufacturing in the volume required to get this toothbrush to thousands of stores. Oral-B was also committed to making great products that would further support its reputation among customers as an innovative company. To let a product out of the stable without enough consideration and design refinement, the Oral-B executives understood, might not only lose money in manufacturing and delivery but also tarnish the company's carefully honed reputation.

Oral-B tooled four of our recommended design variations. This enabled the company to easily build hundreds of production-quality prototypes that could be put in the hands of customers for side-by-side testing. This additional prototyping, what we call a *validation step*, helped us better understand some elements of consumer behavior and preference that weren't obvious at first.

Our new toothbrush had a fat handle to fill out your hand and provide greater control. But it thins down between the thumb and forefinger to allow easily spinning of the brush to reach different sides of different teeth. We originally assumed that the cross section through this thin spot should be cylindrical to facilitate spinning. What we learned after exercising the design was that a cross section with a shape that was closer to square is better at telling the fingers where the bristles are pointed.

You might think this is a seemingly minor design detail, but it's just the kind of detail that adds up to making a "good enough" product great. It's the design difference that sells more toothbrushes for a higher price, builds empathy with consumers, and makes them come back for your toothbrush when they need a replacement.

Another detail we had to consider was all those thin toothbrush holders in millions of bathrooms in American homes. Would they not be rendered useless by the arrival of our fatter model? Oral-B wondered about that, too. We always listen intently to what our clients say, but in this case we advised ignoring the worries about too thin toothbrush holders. Arrogant? Perhaps. Yet we reasoned that this was such a great new product and design that a bigger holder would follow the fatter toothbrush.

This is an important lesson worth expanding on. Sometimes it is necessary to let go of a design constraint in order to make a remarkable product. We looked at toothbrush designs that would fit into conventional holders, but they were all missing the elements that were helping the new design really stand out. The fat-and-thin profile of the toothbrush was the defining design detail that made it so comfortable and visually different. The profile was also at odds with the requirement to fit into conventional holders. Something had to give, and in this case, Oral-B recognized that an opportunity to shine in the market trumped everything else. I'm happy to report from the trenches of the toothbrush wars that the Oral-B CrossAction toothbrush, introduced in 1998, was a huge hit. Exact figures are not available, but the *Los Angeles Times* reported in 2000 that Oral-B had increased its market share to 30 percent from 25 percent of the then $650 million annual toothbrush market within two years. As of 2012, the toothbrush is still in production—further testimony to the benefits of designing a great product.

> Sometimes it is necessary to let go of a design constraint in order to make a remarkable product.

Oral-B did spend $54 million on CrossAction ads, but this winning product wasn't solely the result of an effective advertising and marketing campaign. It came about through intensive design research and prototyping that led to a great product for the customer and a big boost for the bottom line. Any company can have this kind of win if it is committed to design, even if the product (a humble toothbrush) might not seem the most likely candidate for a full-blown design investigation and makeover.

By focusing on the product instead of simply pouring more money into branding and advertising, Oral-B bested the competition in the battle for customer allegiance. This is the same strategy that Apple has used since the days of the Apple II. If you make the best product out there, it will pay dividends well beyond what the equivalent advertising dollars could buy you, because, as we have seen, the product is everything.

Tom Peters, author of the seminal 1982 book *In Search of Excellence* (and also our neighbor at LUNAR's Palo Alto office), has always been a big fan of design. He particularly likes the CrossAction toothbrush, and he must have had it in mind when he told the @Issue Journal of the Corporate Design Foundation about making design the *center* of product development rather than an afterthought. "Mistake No. 1 is treating design as a veneer issue rather than a soul issue. The dumbest mistake is viewing design as something you do at the end of the process to 'tidy up' the mess, as opposed to understanding that it's a 'day one' issue and part of everything."[4]

QUALITY

For many years General Motors' Pontiac division perpetuated an unfortunate mismatch between the brand's marketing pitch and the product. Pontiac's advertising promised drivers the kind of "excitement" that would make their hearts race and eyes dilate, as their high-performance sports cars hugged the road at high speeds and turned heads. The stark reality, though, was that year after year Pontiac delivered economy cars with more horsepower and trendy, short-lived styling. There wasn't much excitement at all,

THREE

except perhaps in the Pontiac ads. For the most part, the cars were wholly unremarkable. They lacked quality.

Consider one entry called the Pontiac Aztek, launched in model year 2001. This clunker was a midsize crossover vehicle targeting a twentysomething market, but it looked like a soccer-mom wagon pretending to be a youthful camper. The idea was to marry some SUV features, such as seating height and cargo space, with carlike handling and fuel economy. The Aztek was promoted as an ultraversatile vehicle that could even turn itself into a sleeping tent for the ultimate camping trip. This was a new category of car. Moreover, it was an amazing development in that GM is not particularly known for innovation.

Even so, it was a mystery to me why Pontiac was the right brand to innovate or why the Aztek ended up looking like the love child of a minivan and a garbage truck. There was near universal agreement about its bad looks. *Time* magazine derided the Aztek as one of the worst cars *of all time*. "The Aztek design had been fiddled with, fussed over, cost-shaved and otherwise compromised until the tough, cool-looking concept had been reduced to a bulky, plastic-clad mess. A classic case of losing the plot,"[5] the magazine wrote in a searing rebuke. In another bad move, this otherwise breakthrough car idea was dropped onto a minivan chassis. That single decision saddled the car with a minivan-like appearance that no amount of body sculpting could hide.

There's an old saying in the product design world: A camel is a horse designed by committee. The Aztek proves the truth of that. Aztek had no singular vision, and so it acquired the various attributes of everyone who touched it. I can almost hear the

There's an old saying in the product design world: A camel is a horse designed by committee.

The Pontiac Aztek—with its flat sides, humped back, and two sets of grilles—was saddled by compromises that watered down the original vision for the car. *Image: General Motors, LLC* committee members talking about their strategy: Save money by using an existing platform. Reduce the size of the tires to reduce gas mileage. Wrap it in plastic to make it look rugged. The result was a crappy design owned by no one because everyone involved in the development process designed it.

After four years of trying to recoup its investment Pontiac pulled the plug on the Aztek. By 2010 GM shuttered Pontiac entirely. The slumping economy was surely partly to blame, but it was also due to how badly Pontiac, a brand first launched in 1926, had failed to live up to its own advertising image as a carmaker supposedly dedicated to high-quality and charismatic vehicles that provide owners with an exciting ride.

Any number of corporate pressures and constraints can lead to an Aztek-like debacle in any industry. I hear complaints from clients all the time about these pressures—ranging from cost controls to managing capital investments, business cycle downturns, cutthroat competition, and regulatory considerations. These are just a few of the myriad issues that can easily preoccupy any company and divert attention from focusing time, attention, and resources on designing a great product.

Apple, of course, isn't immune to these constraints. At times it, too, has succumbed to the "good enough" weakness. In 1993 Apple launched Newton, a product that was well ahead of its time. Newton was a handheld computer that would fit in your pocket (should you have extra large pockets). Its primary innovation was a promise to interpret your natural handwriting. Rather than using a keyboard, the advance here was that you could merely use your handwritten scrawl to schedule a meeting, make a note, or write an e-mail. Could there be a better Apple product? Newton promised to take the natural human skill of writing and convert that to the digital domain.

Bidding good-bye to the keyboard sounded like a great idea. The problem was that Newton was working just fine in the lab but not on the portable hardware itself, according to Tesler, who led the Newton development team, and Alan Kay, another interface guru at Apple who had often dropped in on the project to critique its design. Newton had issues. It wasn't powerful enough. It didn't sync properly with the desktop computer.

But because Apple was in a horserace with Microsoft and with a company called GO Computing to bring such a product to market, it rushed in with a device that was a first try. In other words, a product that was just good enough. In a desperate bid to be first, Apple didn't allow the technology time to catch up with the promise of an integrated desktop and portable experience. And it paid the price. Newton was shipped before its technology was ready, which led to jokes like this one about the glaring inaccuracies of its handwriting interpreter:

Q How many Newtons does it take to change a lightbulb?

A Foux! There to eat lemons, axe gravy soup.

Apple continued to invest in Newton for the next three years, trying to correct the initial missteps, until Jobs finally killed it in 1998, shortly after his return to the company. One of the most astounding things about the Newton flub was that Apple had had another option. Joy Mountford, an early Apple user interface manager, had advocated another approach to the personal digital assistant (PDA), the term that CEO John Sculley created to describe the device. Leaving out the troublesome handwriting recognition piece, Mountford recalled in an interview with me, Apple could have delivered a quality PDA.

Every manager is under pressure and timeline demands to rush out mediocre products like the Newton. Development teams

The natural handwriting recognition software in the Apple Newton worked great in the lab on powerful computers, but was a disappointment on the shipped product. *Image: Grant Hutchinson*

will often acquiesce to a "good enough" product because there is money to be made (at least in the short term) with "good enough." Great is so often the enemy of good. Great costs more and requires more energy and effort. A company can subsist on good enough products. But in the long run, "good enough" will damage everything: your products and your brand and eventually your company, which will also be perceived as just good enough rather than great.

One way that Apple manages to create insanely great products in terms of quality is by selectively limiting the functionality that it promises to deliver, much like we did for Oral-B in giving up on the conventional toothbrush holder. The first iPhone was insanely great even though it lacked some functionality you might have expected in a smartphone. All those apps couldn't be organized into folders. You couldn't switch between apps running at the same time. No picture taking with a locked phone. Did the geniuses at Apple have a momentary lapse and just forget about these features? Not likely. They know that packing too much functionality into a product at the start will mean either missing the launch date or giving up on quality. And they know that there's time to add functionality into the product in updates. In the first iPhone launch in 2007, Apple didn't go after the business user as much as entertainment-focused customers, who were delighted with the product.

REPETITION

If you continually design quality products, then each successive one benefits from and adds to the greatness of the one that came before. The first iPhone in 2007 was a sales megahit (up to 700,000 units in the first weekend alone, according to estimates) and so was the iPhone 4S, released in late 2011 (4 million units sold in the first weekend). This despite the fact that the iPhone 4S wasn't a great leap forward technologically—except for Siri, the built-in personal concierge—and initially debuted with less-than-stellar reviews. More important than the number of new features, though, is the quality of how those new features are implemented.

A basic tenet of Apple's success is that consistency propels a brand forward. The effect of repetition is like a flywheel. I can explain.

A flywheel is a nifty moving component of many machines. It's merely a heavy wheel that is hard to get moving, but once it gets going, the flywheel stays spinning and keeps things running smoothly. Think of your brand as that flywheel. Its speed represents the impact of marketing on all of your products, services, advertising, and any other touch points. Each new product has a huge potential to make the flywheel spin faster or to slow it down.

If you continually design quality products, then each successive one benefits from and adds to the greatness of the one that came before.

Advertising can also speed up or slow down the flywheel, but these days it has a much smaller effect on the flywheel than does a great new product. Great products create momentum in the flywheel because customers develop trust in your brand and spread its greatness by word of mouth, propelling the flywheel even faster. Taking the metaphor one step further, when your brand flywheel is moving very fast, it's easier to convert new customers because the trust in the brand reputation is very high.

While Apple had a sterling reputation in the early 1990s for building remarkable products compared to much of the competition, the launch of the ill-fated Newton endangered its reputation as a leader. The Newton slowed down the Apple flywheel. So did MobileMe, an early cloud computing service launched in 2010 that was criticized for numerous and embarrassing technical snafus. It just didn't work. Apple had screwed up. But did it stop the fast-spinning Apple flywheel? Not at all. Apple had already created a very fast flywheel of a brand with the iMac, iPod, and iTunes. The problems with MobileMe were a relatively a rare but glaring and unexpected glitch that didn't stop Apple's flywheel because it is a company that repeats its quality formula so well.

The flywheel analogy works the other way, too. If your company has consistently offered unremarkable products, when a great one comes along it won't move the needle much in the marketplace. This hasn't stopped any number of companies from spending vast amounts of money on designing one-hit wonders, as Motorola did with the RAZR V3. Or what Pontiac tried to do with a two-seater ragtop sports car called Solstice that it introduced in 2004.

Unlike Pontiac's doomed Aztek, the Solstice received impressively warm accolades from the automotive press. Its design was more like an attractive British-made roadster than an ungainly American muscle car. "What a beauty," concluded Roger Martin, dean of the School of Management at the University of Toronto and a popular design advocate, after getting behind the wheel. "A drop-dead gorgeous convertible roadster listing at a mere $19,995. [It's] destined to be a hit."[6]

I was also beguiled by Solstice's dashing good looks, while also wondering how it was produced by Detroit. But in the end I didn't buy one. I loved the look of the car, but it still wore the Pontiac badge, the brand with the slow-moving flywheel. In my mind, it would never be as great and lovable as an MG from the 1960s or the Audi TT, which I did end up buying because it is not only a beautiful car but also part of a continuing tradition of great cars and Audi's sophisticated design heritage. It was a great product that simply sold itself.

The Pontiac Solstice, launched in 2006, was a one-hit wonder that failed to carry the brand. *Image: General Motors, LLC*

SUMMARY

The product is the ultimate message and messenger in the Internet age of too much information, where the competition for attention is frantic. Only a truly great product stands out amid the clutter. Traditional advertising and marketing can't make a "good enough" product great; a great product with outstanding design is the best messenger. That product is the primary lens through which the customer sees the company and brand, and what customers want to see is quality, again and again. Repeating quality reinforces the design values and creates customer appreciation and loyalty.

THE BUILDING BLOCKS

Message is what your product or a succession of products says to customers and what it means to them cumulatively over time.

Quality design elevates a product from the ordinary and unremarkable to extraordinary and outstanding. By focusing the function of the product and even narrowing your market and marketing requirements, you can overcome the tyranny of good enough and create products that are great.

Repetition of message and quality in new and innovative products, or even incrementally better ones, reinforces a product's design credentials and solidifies the company brand and image as dependable in the customer's mind.

DESIGN LIKE APPLE AGENDA

Before we discuss the concept of the context in which your products live, let's review the lessons of this chapter by asking questions about your products and whether they qualify as great:

1 Where do your products rank on the "purple cow" spectrum? Are they bland and anonymous, or are they colorful standouts in the crowd? Can customers really see them amid the clutter?

Are your products clunkers, like the Pontiac Aztek ,or hits, like an Oral-B toothbrush? To design like Apple, acknowledge that the product is the best message and messenger of your brand and company.

2 Are your advertising and marketing efforts focused on your product? Devise advertising and marketing campaigns to augment the great product rather than wasting money trying to elevate a "good enough" product to great with a bigger ad budget. Don't fall for empty-messaging ad campaigns, like the Dancing Elf, that fail to differentiate your product from the herd.

3 Do you seek greatness in all of your products? Or do you strive only for the occasional great one, like Pontiac's Solstice roadster? A one-off great product doesn't have the oomph to get the flywheel spinning faster to reinvigorate your brand or change its image.

4 Are you defining product functionality too broadly, trying to be all things to all people? Focusing on fewer functions can result in better products, because your team will be able to concentrate on solving the right problems. The Oral-B CrossAction toothbrush was a hit even though it didn't fit in conventional toothbrush holders.

5 Does your company repeat greatness with a string of outstanding products? Keep the flywheel spinning for the brand and company by always repeating quality in successive generations of the product (e.g., Apple's iPad 2012 or the iPhone 4S). Repetition with a family of great products will create a unique and enduring relationship with the customer.

Design Is Systems Thinking

Product and context are one.

In 1969, Sony introduced the Digimatic clock radio, an analog clock in a neat rectangular wooden box with a digital-like display featuring flipping numbers. It looked great on a night table. A decade later, Sony scored again with the Walkman, the portable cassette player that prompted a music revolution, of sorts. It wasn't necessarily a technological leap, because portable tape recorders were already available, and Sony simplified the portable tape recorder by taking out the option to record anything. But Sony smartly marketed the Walkman to ordinary folks as a device that let you take your music anywhere. Sound familiar? It's a concept that Steve Jobs and Apple would later exploit with the iPod.

We know what happened to Apple. But where did Sony's innovative streak take the company? For a number of reasons, Sony gradually lost its way after the Walkman because it lost touch with what customers wanted. Sony made no effort to integrate hardware and software, or move toward convergence of content and services, the defining trend of the Internet era. By early 2012, Sony had become a marginalized player. And after four straight loss-making years and its stock at a two-decades' low, the *Wall Street Journal* noted that "Sony is struggling to match the speed and production might of Samsung Electronics or deliver the category-defining innovations of Apple."[1]

While Sony has struggled, Apple started 2012 with its stock at an all-time high. Its market value surged to over $400 billion, bringing it neck and neck with the oil giant Exxon. Apple's cash horde totaled over $100 billion. Of course, it was great products and premium prices that helped swell Apple's bottom line. Yet the foundation of Apple's financial success is also based on its ability to link products to the experience around it and to sell all the other stuff related to that experience. Apple makes money off the product as well as the context that surrounds the product. Instead of churning out dozens of look-alike products for narrowly defined markets, Apple brings out only a few great products and extends the context around them with more products and services in what is euphemistically known as the iUniverse.

That universe never stops expanding. By the first quarter of 2012, Apple had sold more than 25 billion apps from its App Store. More than 16 billion songs had been downloaded from iTunes (a number that CEO Tim Cook gleefully compared to the 220,000 Walkman cassette players that took Sony 30 years to sell). All those beautifully designed Apple products were being sold in more than 300 beautifully designed Apple Stores worldwide. The context and the experience are the ways Apple keeps itself

The Sony Digimatic clock radio was one innovation in a series of big winners for the company from the 1950s to the 1980s. *Image: Courtesy of Sunday Drive Vintage, Amy Jung* situated directly in front of the customer—in the fabled catbird seat—because the customer not only needs the product but all things related to it.

Creating context is not an idea that originated with Apple, although in my mind it has shrewdly elevated context to a new and lucrative level. In an early iteration of the concept, Eliel Saarinen, the influential twentieth-century modernist architect, put it this way, "Always design a thing by considering it in its next larger context—a chair in a room, a room in a house, a house in an environment, an environment in a city plan."[2] He was describing the way an architect thinks about context when designing a building, as well as the intrinsic, interlocking relationships that exist between the smallest components and the space around it in ever-expanding circles. Apple took that idea, which I call *zooming out,* and ran with it. Zooming out and away from a problem to see the bigger picture is an activity that takes place in the right brain, the home to most creative thinking. The opposite of that is *zooming in,* which lets you observe the smallest details of a problem in seeking a solution.

SYSTEM DESIGN

Apple orchestrates every small detail that contributes to how the customer perceives the product, from the perfect packaging to the interior design of its retail stores, where free-floating glass staircases and color-coordinated T-shirts worn by the staff are all part of the carefully constructed environment. Apple zooms in to see the immediate world adjacent to the product and then zooms out to see the wider circles emanating from the product, all from the customer's perspective and point of view. In this way, Apple observes the system in its entirety.

The challenge for any company is how to bring together, from the many different voices and departments in an organization,

FOUR

a unified vision that leads to a cohesive product experience. Customers expect to have one fluid experience and not a disjointed mishmash of garbled messages and overlapping or indistinct points of view. How do you choreograph the disparate demands and priorities so the result is a holistic, systematic design that blends the critical touch points around the products and services?

Eliel Saarinen's mandate to design within a context is a good starting point. At my firm, we begin by asking our clients about their objectives in order to understand what the product is meant to be and what they hope it will mean to their customers. Identifying the right questions is often more important than designing the product. Questions help us zoom out to Saarinen's levels of larger and larger context. Our work with Palm Computing is a good way to illustrate how we ask questions as the first step to find a solution.

Questions help us zoom out to Saarinen's levels of larger and larger context.

In 1996, Palm launched the PalmPilot, a first-generation, handheld personal digital assistant (PDA). Three years later Palm asked us to design a new product for the company. The project brief was simple: To gain market share Palm, wanted its lineup to include a new device at a lower price. The team at Palm told us that their market was mostly made up of mobile business professionals and that this new product would target that segment, too, but cost less than their other products that ranged in price from $250 to about $500. Palm explained its value proposition and unique design philosophy. Counter to what the Apple Newton and Microsoft's Windows CE were doing in the space, Palm had created an organizing principle called the "Zen of Palm." Not surprisingly, the watchwords of Palm's creed were simplicity and ease of use. While rivals were trying to pack features

Zooming out and considering the evolving context of the Palm market led to a new framework that positioned a new, low-end product in a formerly untapped consumer market space. *Image: LUNAR*

PALM PRODUCT OPPORTUNITY FRAMEWORK

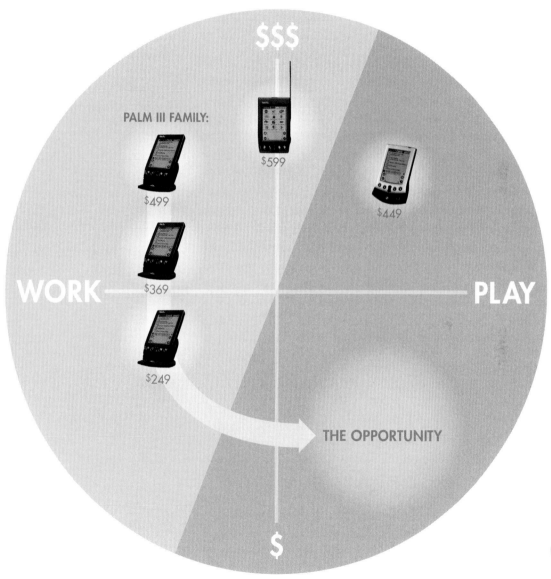

$$$

PALM III FAMILY:

$499

$599

$449

WORK — $369 — PLAY

$249

THE OPPORTUNITY

$

into their PDAs, Palm expressly wanted to take features *out*. The result: Palm's handheld computers were faster and simpler, yet still packed a punch, with great functionality that people needed and appreciated while on the go.

We immediately zoomed out to see where this new product would fit with Palm's other offerings. We posed this question: How will this new product relate to the other products in the Palm lineup? Saarinen would have been proud. The team at Palm unfolded their road map, which was a classic list of products plotted on a timeline. The road map included current products, their target "sunset dates," and projections about products that were in development. One of the current products was the Palm V model. With its metallic shell and slim design, the Palm V was gaining in popularity with business executives for more than purely functional considerations. The Palm V was taking on a new meaning and evolving into a status symbol. It was attracting buyers who were interested not only in functionality but also in a golf-club, jet-set lifestyle. We asked more questions to get a better grip on the context of the market. What might a business customer want in a cheaper, stripped-down PDA? What is happening more broadly in the design of PDAs? How might Palm reach more customers with this new device? And zooming out even further, we wondered whether this new entrant at the low end would appeal to people's lifestyle choices rather than only to their business needs.

To help answer these questions, we reconstructed the Palm product road map in the shape of a target that described its product opportunities laid out in a two-dimensional market space. In the vertical direction, we plotted against the product price point. In the horizontal direction, we plotted how the product would be used: for organizing work activities at one end, or for ordering a customer's personal life at the other. Looking at the

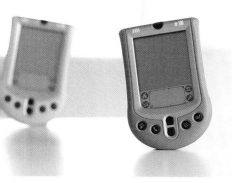

target, we realized that most of Palm's products were moderately expensive work tools, but the showy new Palm V was charting a new path as a pricey executive assistant, bridging professional and personal uses. At the bottom of the market space where the prices are lowest, the products—with their limited performance and lower cost—become more attractive to consumer purchasers rather than professional ones. What's more, there was no viable competitor occupying that rich, untapped space at the low end, where moms and students were the target customers.

This new framework helped define the context of Palm's products and inspired the team to design the Palm m100, a PDA that purposefully incorporated lifestyle cues to appeal to new customers. Its profile featured a rounded bottom and a graspable waist, attributes that gave the design a friendly and approachable look. Moreover, the m100 could be customized with personal expressions. Is that dark gray faceplate too boring? Too Wall Street? For $20 you can replace it with a sexier accessory faceplate covered in leopard spots. The model also had what we call "thumbnail equity," meaning that even at the size of a thumbnail ad, the Palm m100 would be recognizable on discount store fliers that come in the Sunday newspaper.

Allow me to gloat here by saying that the m100 was a big hit in all the ways we had predicted, leading Palm chief executive Carl Yankowski to comment in a press release shortly after the product launch, "The volume in the global m100 launch was extraordinary.... [T]his product is reaching well beyond the mobile professional and early adopter. Early market research indicates we've tapped into the student population in a very big way."[3]

This product was so successful that Palm quickly adopted the two-market strategy and created two separate brands, Tungsten and Zire, to carry it forward. Tungsten was designed for the alpha crowd of bold productivity users and marketed with the

The result of Palm's reframing was the m100, a product that appealed to students and moms. *Image: Sandbox Studio*

FOUR

catchphrase "Critical Work Gets Done." Its sister brand, Zire, was heralded by the softer line, "Mom Gets Organized."

CREATING EXPERIENCES

To better explain how companies zoom out, let me make a quantum leap from Saarinen's high modernism to IKEA, the global Swedish home-furnishings retailer that is known as much for its low prices and oddly named products as it is for the quality of its in-store customer experience.

Step into any IKEA store in Brooklyn or Kuwait or Singapore and you enter a world specifically designed to immerse the customer in the IKEA home decor universe. You snake your way along a predestined path, passing through meticulously arranged rooms where IKEA products—the sofa, the chair, the rug, and the bookshelves—are laid out as if a real person or family lived there. As you stroll by and visit these miniworlds, with the soft lighting and family photos on the wall and artfully placed objects, you see how these "people" live and how the IKEA products are part of their lives and contribute to their well-being. Products are placed in their context to help you understand the experience of IKEA living at your home.

In a similar way, Virgin Airlines has created a more pleasant flying experience, quite an accomplishment at a time when any air travel is pure drudgery. Virgin tries to minimize the pain with touches such as an amusing animated in-flight safety announcement and allowing passengers to order food and drinks via individual touch screens (attendants deliver the orders so trolleys don't clog the aisles). The pilot steps out of the cockpit to introduce the crew and deliver the predeparture announcement. There's little that can be done to relieve the general awfulness of a cramped seat and a crowded plane, but these touches do soften the rough edges of long-haul misery,

Virgin America uses design to create a comprehensive and differentiated customer experience, from this nightclub mood in their planes to the safety announcement video. Flight attendants on Virgin never slam the overhead bins. *Image: Virgin America*

96

because Virgin took the time to redefine the customer experience and everything that goes with it.

It's a different ballgame, of course, with technology products, but the same design rules apply. First, you must see the world through the lens of the customer to discern needs (more about that in Chapter 6) and then create a product that addresses those needs. The experience follows. That might sound like a logical approach, but many companies routinely ignore it. Think about your own organization: Is product development based on a zoom-out view, taking in the context in which the product will exist? Or does the product sit alone and isolated, unconnected to a wider world of customer needs and expectations?

A company called Dropbox designed its software product, an Internet cloud service, using a very broad context. I discovered Dropbox while writing this book, because I needed a reliable way to back up my notes, manuscript, and book design concepts so they wouldn't get lost. As we all know, accidents happen.

Dropbox almost magically copies files from your computer onto a server at a remote location. This file synchronization happens in the background: The Dropbox software takes care of keeping the files updated—and even lets you know which files have been updated and which ones will soon be. If my computer were to be lost or destroyed (a very real possibility for an absentminded guy like myself), the files would be safe, backed up, and retrievable from any other computer.

The other ingenious thing about Dropbox is that you can access any stored files from other computers or devices, like smartphones and tablets. While on the road without my computer, I have pulled up the manuscript for this book on my iPhone. Impressed with the kind of gee-whiz technology that makes me feel like James Bond, I kept happily uploading big files, such as my notes and curriculum for the class I teach at Stanford, until I overflowed the limit of Dropbox's free storage offering. The time had come to consider signing up for the $10 Dropbox subscription to get more storage. But before doing that, I asked our IT group about other options.

"Look into Microsoft Windows Live Mesh with SkyDrive," the tech wizards suggested. "They give you more space in their free version than Dropbox gives you in theirs, and it's more secure than Dropbox." I decided to give it a try. Yet even before I fired up my Internet browser to give Live Mesh plus SkyDrive a test drive, a strange sinking feeling entered my designer brain. With that mocking Microsoft packaging video in mind, I asked myself: Why does a simple cloud service require five brand names (Microsoft, Windows, Live, Mesh, SkyDrive)? I was already feeling guilty for even thinking about abandoning Dropbox, with its short and punchy name.

Then a second warning flashed. Windows Live Mesh requires you to use that Windows Live account that you probably opened in 2006 to use Windows Messenger at work. What I learned next was that because I hadn't used the account in so long I didn't know that someone in Brazil had been pretending to be me on Windows Live. Being secret agent 007, I could work some magic with the software, and I managed to force a reset of the password to gain access. Next I downloaded the Windows Live Mesh program and installed it on my computer. I opened the application and, through some pretty simple steps, designated the folders I wanted to synchronize with SkyDrive (a pretty good name, I must admit, for a cloud storage system). As things started to sail along, my pessimism abated. A reasonable solution to my free backup challenge was at hand.

That hope was short-lived. Hours later, the application gave me conflicting reports on whether the sync had worked. In the meantime, I had installed the Windows SkyDrive app on my iPad. From the app on the iPad I couldn't view the files that I had synchronized with my SkyDrive account. I Googled for help and found an answer on Microsoft's website. Well, sort of. To my astonishment, I discovered that there are actually two SkyDrives: one that works with Live Mesh and another that you must manually push files to. The Live Mesh version is not accessible from the iPad app.

Let me recap: Two SkyDrives? Five brand names? A service that works on one device but not another? This was a design (and customer experience) nightmare. In a fit, I uninstalled the Live Mesh and SkyDrive software and went back to Dropbox, apologizing profusely to the company for my brief disengagement. I suspect that you have had similar encounters with a product or a service that just doesn't work and drives you batty with frustration. Back in the safe arms of Dropbox, my conclusion is that it's well worth it to pay a modest subscription fee for the simplicity and convenience of a well-designed software-based service to avoid the mental agony of one that is poorly designed.

Microsoft's cloud service is okay, or "just good enough," because it works and backs up files to a virtual Internet-based storage system. But as its lengthy moniker suggests, Microsoft Windows Live Mesh with SkyDrive baffles and frustrates the customer. Unlike Dropbox, IKEA, Virgin, and, of course, Apple, Microsoft often can't see the forest for the trees when it comes to the customer experience. With the SkyDrive product, Microsoft failed to conceptualize the service through the *lens of the customer*.

Dropbox has proved to be a winner. As of 2012, it had signed on over 50 million users. According to a *Forbes* magazine story, Steve Jobs was so impressed with the service that he personally approached Dropbox founders Drew Houston and Arash Ferdowsi with an $800 million offer to buy the company.[4]

They turned him down. In 2011, Apple started its own Internet-based storage service with the fabulously simple name iCloud. It shifts the digital hub of your Apple system to the cloud from the PC, which had been the center for all things Apple, like the iPod and its digital music world.

Once again, we see the stark differences between the Apple and Microsoft design strategies. Microsoft tends to chase market share with any old thing it can get out the door, bugs and clumsy name and all; Apple aims higher, with the best-designed product and a rewarding and simple customer experience. And, as we have seen, the market share naturally follows.

PERPETUAL PLATFORMS

As long as we're zooming out, I'd like to take the discussion of context a step further, to the concept of designing platforms. Platforms are foundational products or systems that can be enhanced by either customers or other commercial partners. The personal computer is a platform. Facebook is a fantastic and durable platform, because it becomes a staging area for all of the things we share with our friends (and others). By using Facebook, we merge our lives with the platform, because the pictures and messages we post are part of the fabric of our social connections, and these are encoded in each friend's user list.

One can argue that Microsoft built a stronger platform in personal computers than Apple did because it established strong partnerships through its more open and flexible licensing model (compared to Apple's so-called walled garden). Even in 2012, the global share of Microsoft Windows based–PCs outpace Apple's Mac by 14 to 1.[5] Microsoft's partners—from PC manufacturers to software application makers—have built businesses to work with the Windows platform, which in turn has led to a very strong business with an enormous installed base. In the Microsoft example, the platform enables the partnerships and the partners empower the platform.

When Jobs returned to Apple in 1997, one of his first public moves was to get Microsoft to endorse the Mac as a viable platform that it would continue to support. It was a surprising reversal for Jobs, who disliked Microsoft and was not usually one for changing. But it was an important signal to the world that the Mac would have partners contributing to the Mac platform. Despite Jobs's preference to control every aspect of the computer experience—integrating hardware and operating system and software—he must have realized that Apple needed customers to believe that the Macintosh would run a range of software that people wanted to use.

In fact, according to Randy Battat, an Apple marketing executive who worked there in the 1980s and 1990s, the original Macintosh struggled for a long time because it was unable to run a rich suite of applications. "The joke at the time," Randy told me in an interview, "was that the Mac ran six programs: MacWrite, MacDraw, MacWrite, MacDraw, MacWrite, and MacDraw." Jobs finally acknowledged the problem and let himself zoom out, knowing that he needed a platform approach to succeed and that rebuilding a relationship with Gates and Microsoft was the only way to go.

Jobs zoomed out again with the iPod and iTunes system. Because managing music on a small, portable device was awkward, Apple put more control of the music library and playlists on the PC in the form of iTunes, where people have a large screen, a keyboard, and a mouse to manage it all. Not unlike Facebook, this little system was starting to become a platform, because people began using it to manage all their music. Apple didn't stop there, of course. Jobs expanded the platform by signing deals with the major record labels to sell music through the iTunes store in a proprietary format. The foundation of the platform was customers using iTunes to collect music, build playlists, and enjoy their music in whatever way they pleased. Once you have your music loaded, located, and organized in the iTunes universe you're not likely to switch to another system. You are a happy camper, listening to your favorite tunes within the smoothly functioning iTunes universe.

Another blockbuster platform is the iPhone and the app phenomenon. In fact, the iPhone is the ultimate platform, because it is virtually a blank slate that customers personalize with the features and capabilities that they want most. With apps, that is. As you know by now, there are apps for everything under the sun, and each one creates another partnership with another company, which is helping Apple by deepening the customer commitment to the platform. Each app creates a stronger bond with the customer, because it further customizes the platform experience. It is now part of Apple lore that Jobs wanted the company

> Once customers have outfitted their iPhone with music, e-books, apps, and perhaps a trendy case befitting a fashionista, they become more than customers. They transform into invested advocates of the product and context and platform.

to write its own apps and initially strongly resisted allowing outside apps to "pollute the integrity" of the iPhone, according to Isaacson. Looking back, it's a good thing (for Apple and for customers) that Jobs decided to open the iPhone to let it become a wider platform.

The platform idea is not limited to music and apps. Jeff Smith, one of LUNAR's founders, likes to think of the physical iPhone as a naked device that begs customers to adorn it with accessories

FOUR

that add individual expression or functionality. There is a huge aftermarket for cases, headphones, speakers, car chargers, credit card readers, docks, and more—all of which expand the universe of partners that support the iPhone platform. Once customers have outfitted their iPhone with music, e-books, apps, and perhaps a trendy case befitting a fashionista, they become more than customers. They transform into invested advocates of the product and context and platform.

SUMMARY

Insanely great products and services are the foundation of success at Apple and other companies. But products do not exist in isolation; they are part of an ever-expanding universe that emanates from the product to the context around it, and spreads from there to systems, experiences, and platforms that surround the customer and create loyalty to the brand. Designers orchestrate these experiences down to the smallest detail by zooming in to closely observe interaction with the product, and zooming out for a panoramic view of the wider context.

THE BUILDING BLOCKS

System design helps companies zoom out to understand their products and services from an observational vantage point and then knit all the pieces together into a cohesive and compelling offering.

Creating experiences is the result of companies zooming out to view the entire system of products in their larger context and designing a holistic response based on how the products fit into the lives, needs, and expectations of real people.

Perpetual platforms are the ultimate product systems because they engage the market commitment of partners who contribute to the platform and the emotional investment of customers, which shifts them from customers to forceful advocates.

1 What are the zoom-in and zoom-out questions related to your company's line of products and services? Is your organization seeing the big picture, or squinting to see only part of the view from above? Take a page from Saarinen to see the connections and relationships between objects and the space around them.

2 Do you understand the context surrounding your products? Can you link products to the surrounding context and understand the opportunities that exist there, rather than the constraints? Consider how Palm found new opportunities by zooming out to reframe its view of the market, where its products would fit, and who would buy the products.

3 Are you considering the whole context and designing a compelling system—or merely a set of products? Follow in the footsteps of Dropbox to design a system that considers the customer context.

4 What are the platform opportunities, whether in partnerships or in customer engagement with your product, service, or brand? Try shifting your thinking from products to services, like Apple did when it moved from music players to the iPod music platforms.

5 Is there a "blank slate" product in your lineup that could serve as a platform and that begs customers to adorn it with accessories? The iPhone is the ultimate naked device yearning for apps to individualize and customize expressions.

FOUR

Design Out Loud

Protoype to perfection.

In 2009, Intel introduced an innovative product called Intel Reader[1], a mobile handheld device for people with reading-based disabilities, such as dyslexia or low vision, or for those who are blind. Simply put, Intel Reader coverts printed text into spoken word. I say innovative not because its component parts were particularly new, but because of how the Reader integrated three existing technologies—the digital camera, optical character recognition software, and a text-to-speech synthesizer—into a groundbreaking advance. Intel Reader provides someone with reading difficulty the ability to hear the contents of a textbook, a phone bill, or a menu. Snap a picture of any of these things and, voilà, Intel Reader tells you what they say.

My colleagues and I at LUNAR were part of the design team for Intel Reader, and a good part of what we did was to prototype. In fact, we prototyped like crazy. While prototyping is an integral part of any design effort, because there was no other product like this one on the market we relied on prototyping to quickly explore a wide range of design alternatives at every stage of development.

A prototype is the tangible embodiment of a future product that helps us get a glimpse of what it will be. Prototypes are the lifeblood of a rich design process, because they stimulate the senses and make concepts real so we can *feel* or *evaluate* the future, whether through our senses and our emotions or through our rational sides, as we invent a new technology. Remember that the design process is neither linear nor predictable. More often than not design is a zigzagging journey of exploration in which the designer must set a course and then take a few detours on the road before reaching the final destination. To a large degree, prototyping is the strongest navigational tool on this journey.

That's why prototyping early in a process is crucial for saving time and resources later in development. There's a saying that floats around the Institute of Design at Stanford (commonly called the d.school). "Fail early to succeed sooner." Had we not prototyped the early designs for the Intel Reader in physical forms, we might have missed the fundamental flaw in the design for days (if not for weeks or months), at which point the cost and delay of changing a design might have put the entire project at risk.

We started quickly and somewhat crudely by creating form factors that approximated digital cameras. After all, the Reader would be first and foremost a camera to capture pages of text. We put together a number of mockups that represented some design ideas, which all looked like large versions of a digital camera: a thin rectangle with a lens on one side and a viewfinder screen on the opposite side. These admittedly rough prototypes were presented to target users in early one-on-one research sessions. What we learned proved to be profound, because we saw right away how people would use the Intel Reader.

With their elbows on the table, the target users supported the camera so that they could take a picture of printed materials resting on the table surface. Two problems were immediately apparent: The users had to cock their wrists awkwardly to angle the camera lens toward the table; and those who could use the viewfinder screen couldn't see the screen because it was pointed at the ceiling! Back at the drawing board, we moved the camera to the bottom of the device, thereby fixing both problems.

This is the power of a prototype. It gets the design out of the heads of individual designers and out where other people can touch it and where designers can see how other people perceive, use, control, enjoy, or struggle with a design. The aim is to let ideas mutate in many directions at once so that the strongest mutations survive. LUNAR designer Ken Wood calls this a process of *directed evolution.* Designers produce a variety of concepts with different traits that are evaluated by the product team. The team will kill concepts that are not fit enough to be carried forward, and the survivors pass on their traits to future designs. Then the process is repeated. The eventual outcome is a product that is strong enough to survive in the real world. Like biological evolution, the offspring of prototypes benefit from previous generations of adaptation. And the more generations there are, the stronger the offspring will be.

As a manager, you might not even know that prototyping takes place, because it is mostly done in the design studio, while you are likely see only the final version of the product. You're probably more familiar with PowerPoint, which one could argue is a prototyping tool. As you know from sitting in untold numbers of meetings, PowerPoint is the primary modeling tool to represent marketing requirements, product specifications, competitive analyses, sales projections, and just about anything else a company needs. PowerPoint decks are useful abstractions

FIVE

A handful of the dozens of prototypes that we used in the development of the Intel Reader. Materials range from paper to Fome-Cor to surfboard foam to three-dimensional printing to Legos—whatever got the job done quickly. *Image: LUNAR*

for explaining the mechanics of a new product or service and for comparing the attributes of the product or service to other company offerings.

But PowerPoint is rarely used effectively as a prototype. Why? Because PowerPoint lacks a real human and emotional connection to the product or service. PowerPoint can describe product features, list channel retailers, and lay out statistics about the demographic makeup of customers, but it can't achieve anything near to what even a simple prototype can, which is to provide a team with a shared vision of the future product or service. Spreadsheets do have their place in corporate decision making, but when talking about future products and services, PowerPoint decks can reflect only a shadow of what the designers are experimenting with. In design circles, we like to say that a picture is worth a thousand words, but a working prototype is worth a million.

Apple uses prototyping more than any other organization that I've ever encountered in my many years as a design professional. Steve Jobs was famous for refusing PowerPoint presentations, because he wanted to see and touch the prototype. He wanted to hold in his hands exactly what his designers were working on, and he liked showing off prototypes to visitors. Jobs made decisions based on touching and playing with the prototype, not by evaluating data and decks and the financial analyses of a PowerPoint presentation.

Walter Isaacson writes in his book that when the first iPad was in development, Jobs and Ive worried over every tiny detail, including what the right screen size should be. "They had twenty models made—all rounded rectangles, of course—in slightly varying sizes and aspect ratios. Ive laid them out on a table in the design studio, and in the afternoon they would lift the velvet

FIVE

cloth hiding them and play with them."[2] Ive is quoted as saying that this painstaking process of prototyping was how they "nailed" the right screen size.

LET'S GET PHYSICAL

Long before I met my wife, I was lamenting to a good friend how hard it was to find people I was interested in dating. "John, you can't steer a parked car," he told me. By that he meant that sitting around and whining that I wasn't meeting anyone I wanted to ask out was tantamount to sitting in a car at the curb without the engine started while expecting to get to any destination. Even going on a date, any date, would create forward momentum that would begin my journey and show me things about people and myself that would help me find my way to new relationships.

I'm not suggesting that dating and marriage can be compared to prototyping a new cell phone, laptop, or toothbrush. But the personal analogy can be applied to the complex and messy process of prototyping and product development. You just have to get off your butt and start doing something. For a designer, that means prototyping.

To explain how prototyping works and which tools and methods you need to know about, let's look at Stanford's design program, where building prototypes is central to design education, because the very act of making things influences how you think about your design. Students at the school are told that theories are welcome as long as the theories are put into a prototype and run through

> There is almost no limit to the forms of a prototype. An important mandate is that prototypes are made in the roughest, fastest form possible while still answering the important questions at hand.

a process shorthanded as "express-test-cycle," or ETC. This was the process we used in the preceding story about the Intel Reader. We expressed our designs quickly as prototypes and then tested them in the hands of users to observe what happened. And we cycled—that is, we repeated the process.

There is almost no limit to the forms of a prototype. An important mandate is that prototypes are made in the roughest, fastest form possible while still answering the important questions at hand. I have seen some wildly simple and effective prototypes in the past couple of years. And I admit that it's often a lot of fun to feel like a kid playing in the sandbox again. For example, one of our designers, Junggi Sung, manipulated a few pieces of paper to show our client, SanDisk, how a magical new flash drive might hide *and* reveal a USB connector (the product was approved on the spot). For a medical client, we deployed Lego models to explore, communicate, and compare different ways that small packets of medicine can be moved through a delivery device. One time, we taped a phone handset to an iPad to start a conversation about the future of tablets and smartphones. We sometimes use videos (rather than models) to illustrate stories about a potential product, as well as three-dimensional printing, which, as the name suggests, is an automatic machine that can create physical objects from computer-aided design (CAD) files through a variety of methods. The machine in our office slices the CAD model up into paper-thin layers and then builds each layer by deposited melted plastic in the shape of that layer. All of these new technologies allow us to prototype even faster and cheaper and more expressively, and that in turn makes it easier for us to imagine the product and explain it to the client.

FIVE

PROTOTYPE AND THE OBJECT

A good way to understand prototyping in the real world is to tell you a story about how we used prototyping to help create a revolutionary joystick for computer games.

In 2004, we were approached by a company called Novint, a spin-off of Sandia Labs. Novint wanted to use newly developed *haptic* technology (i.e., the science of computer-aided touch sensitivity) to create a three-dimensional joystick that would provide gamers a better feel for the action. Expensive haptic systems were already in use by researchers and doctors, who use it to perform minimally invasive surgery with robotic assistance. The leading haptic technology came from a company called Force Dimension, which sold these systems for as much as $20,000. Novint's goal was to come out with a device it could sell for less than $200, and the company asked LUNAR to come up with a great commercial design close to this price point.

Our first prototypes gave Novint and its investors a first peek at what was an exciting, yet nascent, concept. We started with sexy prototypes (we call them *appearance models*) that captured a vision for what the product might become down the road. By sexy, I mean models in translucent white plastic and stainless steel that took their cues from the special effects found in science fiction movies that gamers enjoy. This created a target for what the final product could be and also helped the company build investor enthusiasm around the product idea.

With the Force Dimension technology and our first prototypes in hand, Novint could create a narrative about where it was headed with this product. It was a story that now had some tangible components and emotional appeal, thanks to the physical models prototyped by LUNAR designers. That was a promising start.

Prototypes should be made in the quickest and easiest way possible to make ideas tangible and shareable. This iPad and telephone mash-up provoked a business phone maker to think differently about its opportunities better than an abstract conversation could. *Image: LUNAR*

FIVE

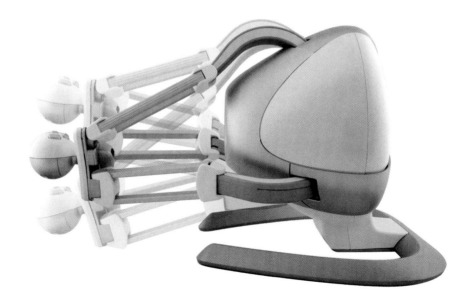

The next hurdle was whether we could make a viable product for Novint's gamer market at a price about 100 times less than what the current haptic technology cost.

To find out, we first confirmed with Asian suppliers that they could provide component parts for a cost within striking distance of the target price. Then we did something nondesigners might consider strange: We tried to make the next prototype a failure. Rather than starting with a design that was dependent on $20,000 technology and trying to whittle that down to the price Novint wanted, we started at the low end and made a prototype in the cheapest way possible. Our "failure" joystick had the cheapest possible components (motors, bearings, and sensors) that we could find or design ourselves. To our complete surprise, this bargain-basement prototype joystick worked remarkably well.

By pushing ourselves to the limit with the cheap parts, we had the chance to back up, or zoom out, and see which components and parts needed further prototyping and adapting. By using the makeshift parts in our prototype, we had learned how to remove a big chunk of the cost. Okay, the cheapo joystick didn't move as smoothly as the high-end product, but we did have a working prototype on the very first go. The real trick was to devise a joystick that fools the hands into believing the gamer is actually touching the action seen on the screen. If at any moment the joystick jitters, wiggles, or responds in a way that is not synchronized with the action on the screen, the gamer's brain will notice, because the human sense of touch is just too sensitive.

Our next design phase involved testing. Walt Aviles, Novint's chief technology officer, who had worked on haptic systems at Sandia, became the human guinea pig for the project, because he could precisely judge the performance. He had a master vintner's "nose," or let's say "hand" in this case. His input fed into refined

Prototypes that were made during the development of the Novint Falcon.
Image: LUNAR

FIVE

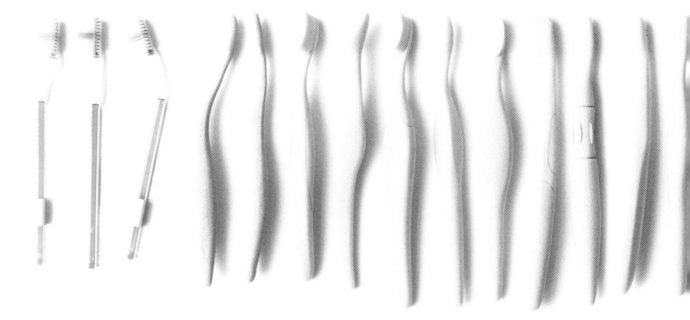

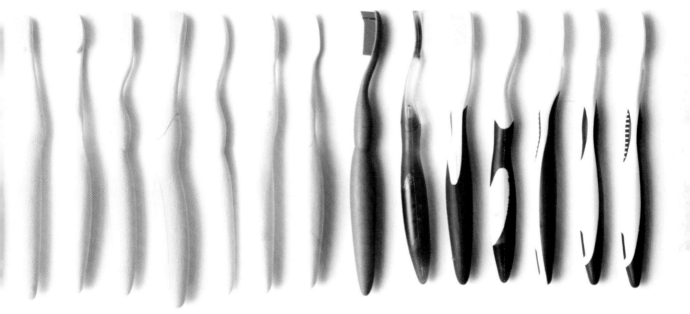

Prototyping was essential to creating a more comfortable toothbrush that would work for the five styles of grip that people use. *Image: LUNAR*

designs from our team and led to a final product that came in on target, price-wise. That eventually became an award-wining product called the Novint Falcon, which has been keeping gamers happy ever since.

Prototyping anchored and guided this product through development. But prototyping isn't limited to a computer, a cell phone, or a joystick. As a manager, you shouldn't dismiss out of hand the concept of prototyping because you think the product isn't worth it or that a low-priced commodity can't benefit from having creative design minds take a whack at making it better. The Oral-B toothbrush we designed not only changed the look of the toothbrush, but also burnished the company's image and brand with a healthy patina of charisma, and also boosted the bottom line. Prototyping helped us to develop the form of the toothbrush that customers would grab off the shelves and killed of those that didn't.

A word of caution for organizations adopting a more design-centered approach to product development. At Apple, the senior team understands prototyping. Novint's leadership did, too. But for organizations new to design, it takes skill to look at prototypes and make a decision based on them. I have seen engineering managers try to kill projects because the prototype was not based on reality. Rather than seeing the *potential* in a prototype, some corporate naysayers see only its faults and judge it as if it were a finished product. This kind of behavior drives designers to hide their work until it's complete enough to be seen by other managers. Another approach I recommend is to make sure that prototypes don't overshoot their intended use. Early prototypes shouldn't look like finished products, because then people will judge them that way. Make them quick and rough, good enough to demonstrate or test the question at hand.

PROTOTYPE AND THE WORKSPACE

At most companies, prototyping takes place in the design studio, because this environment is usually the design and creative hub of the organization. That's the Apple way, too, although exactly what happens inside the Apple design studio remains murky. Given the company's cult of secrecy, access to the studio and information about new products and services are strictly controlled. This is done for obvious reasons, to prevent industrial espionage and, I suspect, as part of the effort to create excitement, buzz, and anticipation about what Apple is up to and what's coming next.

Still, information about the Apple studio sometimes leaks out. I spoke to a person who worked at Apple for almost four years, and her first reaction to a question about the studio was to jokingly compare gaining access to the studio to "the beginning of *Get Smart*," the 1960s television show that spoofed the spy genre and featured a secret headquarters with a vaultlike entrance. Isaacson confirms that impression in his book, writing that the studio is "shielded by tinted windows and a heavy clad, locked door." You might as well try to stroll into the White House. Inside the locked door is a glass-booth reception desk where two assistants stand guard. "Even high-level Apple employees are not allowed in without special permission,"[3] said Isaacson, who did breach the barrier on one occasion.

A person who worked at Apple told me that the mood inside the studio is as one would expect: "peaceful and Zen-like." Product prototypes are strewn across desks, and there are computer-aided workstations, milling machines, and a robot-controlled spray-painting chamber. "There was a sense of joy to be in there and to be working on these things," this

FIVE

person added. In a typically Apple way, however, prototyping doesn't stop at the locked and bolted door. It's a concept that permeates every department at the company. "Protoyping was a way to work through things to try to get to the most compelling truth," the former Apple employee, who worked in the marketing department, recalls. "You have instincts, but you can't always know that right away. It is a process of elimination. [Prototyping] advances the conversation and crystallizes the idea and you come out with a well-thought-through result."

Adam Lashinsky reinforces this by pointing out that every aspect of a product is prototyped at Apple. He relates the amusing story of an unfortunate packaging designer whose job it was to find the best tab "to show the consumer where to pull back the invisible, full-bleed sticker adhered to the top of the clear iPod box."[4] The packaging designer was holed up in a tiny lab with hundreds of prototypes as his quest continued.

Organizations that want to harness more creativity are coming around to the idea that they need to have a space for creative chaos, which we call *designing out loud*.

Not all design studios have Apple's mystical aura. Nor are they always walled-off spaces where designers huddle together, shrouded in secrecy. Designers do often spend days and nights squirreled away at a desk, seemingly oblivious to their surroundings. But design must also be part of a larger organization. Products don't exist in isolation, and neither should the design studio, because design ideas spread virally. As we think about a more collaborative future of work, progressive companies are beginning to look and behave more like design studios. Unlike PowerPoint files, prototypes require space. They tend to be messy. Organizations that want to harness more creativity are coming around to the idea that they need to have a space for creative chaos, which we call *designing out loud*.

This has long been the case at Method Products in San Francisco, where the main workspace is a large open area that Joshua Handy, the company's design director, describes as "a noisy colorful space of products and design and concepts that are out there for everyone to see." Recalling the story about the concentrated laundry detergent the company had developed, Handy says that bags of the detergent and prototypes were lying around the office for years—a constant reminder of an unfinished project and work to be done. Method researchers had been experimenting with pellets as a way to deliver the product, but they couldn't get them to work for a variety of technical reasons. When a colleague of Handy's walked over to his desk to discuss a new pump-bottle idea, the problem and the solution came together in an environment that was conducive to collaboration.

Unlike at Method Products, too many corporate environments resemble sterile cubicle farms with limited collaboration spaces, even in the design studio. Over the past decade, design and architecture firms and design theorists have analyzed the office and how design correlates to productivity, staff retention, and overall happiness. Scott Doorely and Scott Witthoft, codirectors of the environments collaborative at the Stanford d.school, wrote a book called *Make Space* to share their knowledge about designing workspaces that encourage creativity. In a 2012 interview with *Harvard Business Review*'s IdeaCast, they told the host, "We like to have spaces that allow you to materialize your ideas in the lowest, quickest way possible, and that allows you to throw them away when it's time to throw them away." Doorely and Witthoft reckon that space plays a crucial role in how creativity is ignited in individuals and in teams. The very

FIVE

design of a space, the authors argue, can answer questions about where ideas come from and how team members participate in creative development.

Of course, the authors did some prototyping. They discovered that a number of different types of workspaces could help promote idea generation and concept evaluation, as well as prototyping. In 2011, we embarked on a similar experiment with the future of creative work when LUNAR moved into a new facility, a 100-year-old factory building in the Potrero Hill neighborhood of San Francisco.

In designing the space, we intentionally created a number of different workspaces. Square footage was stolen from personal workstations (by pushing desks closer together) to free up some experimental collaboration spaces. Adjacent to everyone's desks are a number of nooks, or small conference rooms, that encourage ad hoc meetings. I like to say that no one has an office but everyone can have one when they need one. Prototyping takes place in a flexible, collaboration laboratory—or co-lab for short—area that is home to the sketches and support material for all current projects. With three variations of space, design teams engage in different ways—from focused individual work to a "designing out loud" project space where prototypes can live adjacent to one another and where creativity flows.

CROWDSOURCED PROTOTYPING

Prototyping doesn't need to take place exclusively in a design studio with designers in charge of the process. It can also flourish in the marketplace by tapping the power of crowds and the people who actually buy and use the product.

Crowdsourced prototyping is most likely to be seen with software development. All of Google's many applications—from

Gmail to Google Docs to Google Calendar—launched in beta form, allowing Google to test-drive these products with millions of users. Google's approach to product evolution is to get an application out there and let the world test it "behind the scenes," although millions of people are doing the testing. Updates to the software happen invisibly to the user. One day the software just gets better, as if by magic. I say "as if," because nobody has to download or install an update.

This is relatively easy for Google to do because of its vast user audience (it logs an estimated 2 billion searches per day). Google can easily select, say, 100,000 users and give them a different version of the software to try out, maybe without even telling them that they are the test rabbits. Google tweaks the width of borders, the size of text, or the color of links as much as it likes to find the most perfect size, color, and proportion. And, of course, this is all tied to its monetization model (what drives you to click more times on the links).

The drawback to prototyping in the real world is that it rarely leads to insanely great products. As a designer, I like and use many Google products. But with the exception of Google Maps—especially its implementation on the iPhone, and the topographical feature that stirs some nostalgic feelings about classical maps—I don't find much inspiration in any of them. Larry Tesler, who is regarded as the father of the graphical user interface for the Macintosh, noted that when companies like Google crowdsource prototyping, it's like tweaking a molehill and hoping it becomes a mountain. But many of these will never become mountains.

In fact, Google killed two products in 2012—Google Buzz and Google Wave—that had been launched with great fanfare just a couple of years ago. It wasn't that surprising. From what I can see, Google asks a lot of questions and does continuous testing on features and functions, but it's not clear who decides exactly what to prototype. It seems like many of Google's products are launched half-baked and then merely modified, or dropped, with a shrug of the shoulders.

In the end, I think Apple's model will prove much stronger. Apple products evolve through rigorous design and prototyping to reach perfection (or pretty near perfection) before they are launched. After that, Apple closely watches how people use them while work continues on the next generation of that product. The crowd is sort of involved, but they are not helping Apple decide between good and a little better. They are informing decisions about tweaking something that is already insanely great.

NEAR-LIFE EXPERIENCES

Prototypes needn't be physical models that you can hold in your hand, or objects that represent a stage in the development and evolution of a future concept or product. Prototypes can be experiences or stories. We all love to tell stories—to ourselves, to our friends, and, of course, to children. Stories help us understand the world and all its complexities and mysteries.

Animated films tell amazing stories, whether hand drawn by the masters in the early days of Disney or by today's digital artists using advanced computer tools at Pixar, the digital-animation company that was owned by Steve Jobs before he sold it to Disney. Yet even with animation technology, you still need stories to animate, and these can be prototyped, too.

Pixar's Academy Award–winning animator John Lasseter, who helped create *Toy Story* and *A Bug's Life*, uses prototyping in every scene in every movie. In his book *The Second Coming of*

Steve Jobs, author Alan Deutschman relates that Lasseter would first sketch out storyboards and then film them, before taking the reel to Jeffrey Katzenberg at Disney. Lasseter would then play the reel "filling in the voices for all of the characters and acting out their movements."[5] Lasseter's talent wasn't just drawing and animating well. He could make "the drawings come alive with vivid characterization," Deutschman writes. Lasseter was developing the plot, characters, and narrative as an experiential or emotional prototype.

As designers, we work with clients to help them get excited about how great their product or service could be. But once in a while, we like to have some fun and tell a story that scares the crap out of them. It's all for their own good, of course.

When Hewlett-Packard shifted in 1999 from being an enterprise and business computing company to being a consumer-oriented computing and printing company, the inkjet printer division asked us to help create a consumer design capability. HP didn't want us to design a new printer. It wanted to know how to reorganize the company and hire the right staff so it would be in a position to create products that would be meaningful to customers.

Part of our solution to this mandate was to create a series of "near-life experiences" as away of prompting gut feelings about how it would feel when new competitors moved into HP's space. We wanted to point out how important it would be for the organization to quickly adopt the consumer design strategy that we were helping it to create. A little playacting would work like shock therapy. Call it design shock therapy.

Fifty HP managers in the company's inkjet division were brought together for a presentation to introduce them to the new consumer design division. During our presentation we

FIVE

flashed on the screen a page purporting to be from *Sony Style*, a magazine that featured a very hip display of Sony products aimed at a younger audience attuned to coolness and charisma. The page in question showed a modern entertainment unit filled with various Sony stereo equipment, including a great-looking Sony inkjet printer in high-polish black right there in the stack. Jeff Smith, LUNAR's founder and the guy giving the presentation said nonchalantly, "… and here is what Sony is doing to leverage its brand and move into your market." There were soft gasps in the room. These marketers and engineers were caught totally off guard by the "revelation" that our designers had concocted and Photoshopped it into

Increasingly, designers and design firms are relying on storytelling or time-based experience prototypes to research and explain how a new system works and impacts real people.

the *Sony Style* page. The HP managers quickly got the point: They needed to act swiftly and decisively to shift their thinking from enterprise customers to consumer customers. Our story embedded a message in a visceral medium that was as targeted and direct as any animated scene presentation John Lasseter would make.

We also use stories to explain, inform, and communicate. In 2011, LUNAR's European office in Munich worked with the German environmental organization Green City e.V. and the University of Wuppertal to design a new system to encourage urbanites to use alternatives means of transportation. The team zoomed away from the problem and identified the issues hindering greater use of bicycles, electrobikes, and trains as "green" alternatives to driving cars in a city with a growing car congestion problem. Research showed, for example, that 80 percent of city residents owned bikes but used them only 10 percent of the time. A new mobility system called mo' (short for mobility) was designed to change user behavior and encourage eco-friendly transportation decisions. There was no better way to explain mo than through videos chronicling how ordinary citizens use the new system throughout their day.[6]

The beauty in this prototype is that it uses stories to communicate a complex experience that changes over time: in this case, different people using alternative transportation for a variety of reasons and situations. It's easy for people to project themselves into the story to imagine themselves climbing on an electrobike or calculating the "mo-miles" they have accumulated while using the system, which makes participants feel like they are part of a special community (mo was designed for Munich but can be applied in any urban area). Increasingly, designers and design firms are relying on storytelling or time-based experience prototypes to research and explain how a new system works and impacts real people. Whether a video, a foam model, or scraps of paper, all prototypes are essential tools that help designers through the process of visualizing and creating a future product or service.

SUMMARY

Prototyping is the lifeblood of a complex design process. It enables designers and managers to make product concepts real and imaginable before they are real. Prototyping involves building the quickest and dirtiest model to do the job—whether paper, cardboard, foam, three-dimensional printed models, videos, storytelling, or near-life experiences—to explain, inform and communicate what a product and service will be.

FIVE

THE BUILDING BLOCKS

Design out loud means an open and shared design and prototyping process in which ideas freely circulate among collaborators and are not locked away in isolation.

Prototype the object is a way to visualize in a multitude of forms and variations what a product might be in order to work through flaws and costs and appearances until all critical parameters are addressed.

Crowdsourced prototyping takes prototyping out of the design studio and into the marketplace to tap the power of the crowd by focusing on people who actually buy and use the product.

Near-life experiences move prototyping from physical objects you can hold in your hands to storytelling and visualized experiences that help us understand how a product or service will work in real situations and impact the target audience.

DESIGN LIKE APPLE AGENDA

Before we examine how to use design to connect with the customer, let's review the lessons of this chapter about prototyping by asking questions about how products and services at your company evolve from an idea to a final version:

1 How do products at your company come into being? Are they dreamed up in the marketing department, or do they start taking shape in the design studio as prototype models? To design like Apple, prototyping is necessary to visualize and imagine the product and to work out kinks and costs long before it is ever manufactured, as exemplified by the Intel Reader and the Novint joystick.

2 Does prototyping take place in a closed or "design out loud" environment? Are design ideas allowed to float and circulate around the organization in a collaborative process? Don't relegate design to a closed space, but open it up to everyone, as Method does.

3 What are the different inputs that influence the process of design and prototyping at your company? Try to use a variety of sources in prototyping. Apple assesses feedback from the marketplace and the tech press, whereas many software makers use crowdsourcing to test applications directly with users.

4 Are you enhancing prototyping with physical objects to include near-life experiences and storytelling videos? Incorporate real stories into prototyping to explain, inform, and communicate ideas about products and services so people can see exactly what the impact will be, whether it's a new line of printers or an alternative transportation system like mo' in Germany.

FIVE

Design Is for People

Connect with your customer.

For me, the allure of design started with cars. When I was 12, I drew cars all the time, fascinated by the look and details of each model. I had a coveted subscription to *Road & Track* magazine, *the* car magazine, which I devoured each time it landed in the mailbox. I knew the name of every production car and even most of the rare supercars from most of the century. I could recognize the illustrators in *Road & Track* before looking at their signatures. And, of course, I also imagined getting behind the wheel. I fell asleep at night imagining myself in any number of crazy adventures that involved driving very fast and guiding my sports car around hairpin turns.

In my doodles I designed sports cars, trucks, and SUVs. I was obsessed with their forms, especially the side view and body and wheels. What I liked most were the European and Japanese cars I saw cruising on the highway, because even at that young age I noticed the different details. American cars were sloppy, overgrown beasts. They had giant gaps between the tires and the wheel wells. The dashboards didn't integrate seamlessly with the door panels. But, oh, a foreign make like a Mercedes or a Mazda, here the design was tighter; the fenders hugged the tires, more like what I saw in racing cars. As an adult and a designer (and still a car freak), I know that it's easy to cut corners and overlook such details.

Looking back on my childhood and obsession with cars, I realize that my infatuation was all about me. I was the center of attention, or in today's marketing jargon, the end user. I wasn't designing to meet the needs of other people. I remember seeing a Chrysler Dodge Caravan, the first minivan that was introduced during my car love period, and couldn't for the life of me make sense of this model's appeal. I hadn't yet developed a designer's keen sensitivity to discovering the needs and desires of *other* people and how to use those insights to create products customers can't live without. To me, the minivan was merely another ugly American car destined for the junkyard.

What I didn't understand was that the minivan was born out of a customer-aware designer insight, which began with a researched understanding of the way that American families were living and where the pain points existed in the current product offerings. This pointed the way to defining opportunities for future products.

Lee Iacocca and his team at Chrysler had a shared understanding of the needs of suburban families that led to the development of the Dodge Caravan— a huge success because of how well it resonated with the target customers. *Image: Courtesy of Chrysler Group LLC*

The minivan let soccer moms effortlessly deliver kids to practice games and birthday parties and to malls and amusement parks. It was easy to drive, easy to load—with plenty of seats for the kids and their friends *and* the dog. The big sliding door allowed parents to buckle up little Janie in the child seat and retrieve the cooler without wrenching their backs. The floor sat close to the ground, making it easy to step in, while the driver sits high with a commanding view of traffic. And the abundance of cup holders meant that everyone could be armed with their morning coffee or their afternoon snack in between school and dance class. The minivan defined a new category that is ubiquitous today because it answers so thoroughly the needs of families with preteen kids (marketers, in fact, now refer to a specific "minivan life stage" to describe this period in an American family).

Even if minivans aren't your thing, for whatever reason, we've all had those *aha* moments of discovery when a new product or service addresses a need we didn't know we had.

Even if minivans aren't your thing, for whatever reason, we've all had those *aha* moments of discovery when a new product or service addresses a need we didn't know we had. It's as if researchers reached into our minds and poked around to find something that was missing. Then they came up with exactly the right thing to scratch an itch we hadn't even felt.

Some examples: TiVo eliminated complex VCR programming and Dropbox simplified file sharing and backup. Quicken brought order to our personal finances, and OXO made vegetable peeling more satisfying. Apple made sense of how we manage our own personal digital music. Observing the lives of customers to find these unmet needs leads companies to create products and services that create new value, whether it's an incremental improvement in an existing product or a big insight that carves out a new market category.

These innovations are not necessarily cutting-edge technology. That OXO vegetable peeler isn't reinventing the wheel or introducing the world's fastest silicon chip. The peeler simply has a great ergonomic handle and a heft and feel about it that seems just right. What OXO and other companies have perfected is a talent for listening, and that connects to a core principle of design: the notion that you're designing for someone else, as the designers at Chrysler did when they conjured the minivan. This is the Apple approach to design. Apple assumes the role of the customer in the design process and considers every aspect about the product, from the user interface to the in-store retail experience when the customer finally comes into direct contact with the product.

Apple, of course, applies that principle to technology, using design to add a distinctly human sensibility. It makes technology feel emotional, as if a friend rather than an infuriating automaton is in the room. In other words, the digital (technology) feels analog (human). With Apple products, technology does its business behind the scenes but is presented to us as facial expressions. When you swipe to the last page of apps on your iPhone, and then keep swiping, the path moves a little bit and then bounces back, in what Apple calls a "rubber band action," to signal that you have reached the last page. Rubber band action is completely unnecessary from a programming perspective, but it makes the experience human and delightful. Apple understands that people are wired to treat complex systems as living beings. We recognize patterns in ATMs and on websites and in retail experiences, because that's just how we are, and these interactions become human ones. "Comcast is not very friendly," we might say. But we're not talking about any individual at Comcast. We're talking about the synthesis of all our Comcast experiences.

That human sensibility applies to the first customer interaction with an Apple product. You take it out of the beautiful box, hit the on button, and start using it without lots of fumbling and decoding of badly written instructions. These products are ready to use even by people who might never have touched one before. They are programmed to smoothly lead customers to their first downloaded e-mail, song, or e-book—which will be the first of many easy and delightful experiences.

A HUMAN CENTERED ETHOS: EMPATHY

In researching this book, I spoke with a number of former Apple employees who helped me construct a firsthand view of the company at every stage of its history. The common thread I detected in all of their stories and comments was that everyone at Apple believes in the company's mission to change the world. That might sound like a pompous and oversized aspiration, but it is taken very seriously by the employees, who share a human-centered ethos, or empathy, which is the ability to understand the feelings of others.

> Everyone at Apple believes in the company's mission to change the world. That might sound like a pompous and oversized aspiration, but it is taken very seriously by the employees, who share a human-centered ethos, or empathy.

It all comes down to details, like the volume buttons on the side of the iPhone. Dozens of prototypes were made just to tune the feel, size, sound, shape, icons, and orientation for those two buttons. Product design engineers know that even these seemingly minor details are part of the human-centered ethos and can make the product feel like a million bucks—or a piece of crap.

You might be wondering at this point how Apple manages to know its customers so well. How does it maintain such high

SIX

customer satisfaction levels *all* the time? What kind of research goes into designing products that inevitably become high-margin profit makers, category killers, and industry game changers all rolled into one? To have that kind of empathy, one assumes that Apple employs thousands of people whose only job is to plumb the depths of customer consciousness so the company has precise information about what products and services will strike deep into the heart of desire.

However, according to executives from Steve Jobs on down, Apple doesn't operate like many other companies in that it doesn't ask the market what to make or undertake conventional forms of research. As discussed in Chapter 2, Jobs distrusted research. Instead of asking customers or the market about products, Apple works largely from intuition and a pervasive human-centered ethos. "We figure out what we want," Jobs told *CNNMoney* in 2011, underscoring the "We design for ourselves"[1] mantra. Instead of focusing on market research or feedback, Apple has established an internal process where design ideas are traded and filtered in the development process, according to one former Apple product design engineer I spoke with.

This concept isn't unique to Apple. Another Silicon Valley giant, Hewlett-Packard, utilized human-centered design decades before Apple did by encouraging its engineers to look over at their colleagues when imagining new products. This practice, dubbed "next bench," was promoted by HP founders Bill Hewlett and Dave Packard and became widespread in the company, as veteran HP designer and LUNAR colleague Shiz Kobara told me in an interview. "Their customers were essentially people just like themselves—engineers at the forefront of technology," Kobara explained. "If the guy at the next bench needed what you were inventing, there was a good chance there was a market for it."

I suspect it's at least partially true that Apple employees are their own best customers. The extremely talented people working there are no doubt an unequaled source of inspiration about products and design refinements. They have amazing intuition about what makes a product—more precisely, an Apple product—click with a customer. Of course, with Jobs at the helm for so long and with his imperious personality, you could say Apple was in fact using "next bench" design for only one person on the next bench (or in the executive suite): That was Jobs, of course, who had discerning design taste and judgment.

The "next bench" concept doesn't always pay off, however. It can create huge problems for companies when the teams are not in tune with the market. Just look at what happened when General Motors and Ford jumped on the Chrysler minivan success bandwagon. Both automakers made the mistake of handing the design challenge to their truck engineers, partly because they wanted a vehicle on the truck line that would help meet federal fuel-efficiency standards.[2] Truck engineers, of course, make trucks, and the resulting minivans they designed were therefore more like trucks—much heavier and harder to handle than the Chrysler models, which stayed true to the goal of being better family cars.

DESIGN RESEARCH

Despite repeated denials by Steve Jobs and others that Apple doesn't do any traditional research, there's no doubt in my mind that Apple does listen to its customers, and that can clearly be labeled as research. When Apple chief executive Tim Cook announced the new iPad in March 2012, he referred to the fact that the company had "talked to customers" about their favorite device for reading and writing e-mail. (It was the iPad. Are you surprised?) It's also clear that Apple pays close attention to what people say about its products via Internet web chatter and social media. While we don't usually consider these traditional research methods, it is a type of research, and whatever information Apple does record is digested and finds it way to subsequent product improvements and revisions.

That iPhone 4S in your pocket has largely the same physical user interface components and on-screen features as the first-generation iPhone. But the details have been enriched. Picture-taking speed has increased, because there's a button on the lock screen that starts up the camera, eliminating several steps in the process compared to previous models. Creating appointments is much faster, because Apple added some much-needed functionality to the calendar app. And, most interesting to me as a designer, the iOS 5 includes features that are seemingly "borrowed" from Google's Android phone—such as the customizable window shade interface that shows the day's weather, events, and stock ticker—even though Jobs had blasted Google for stealing the iPhone interface from Apple. All of these features had been talked about at great length in the press and online and certainly informed Apple's decision to include them in new software releases.

Imagine a coming together of design and the social sciences, in which the designer's inherent capacity to control elements of design converges with the methodologies and strategies social scientists use to uncover the unmet needs of customers.

If your company doesn't follow the Apple top-down approach to design development, research can be a powerful path to creating a shared empathy for customers. I'm not talking about market research, which collects quantitative statistical data from a defined demographic focus group. I'm talking more specifically about *design* research.

Design research takes an anthropological view of the world. It means going into the field to observe and gather qualitative information about people. It means understanding the behaviors and motivations that will be the foundation of an informed design process. Imagine a coming together of design and the social sciences, in which the designer's inherent capacity to control elements of design (form, color, proportion, balance, and flow) converges with the methodologies and strategies social scientists use to uncover the unmet needs of customers.

When we worked on the Oral-B toothbrush project, we looked at videos of real people in their real bathrooms brushing their real teeth. By watching people in context, we had a spy-eye view of their private habits and were able to synthesize some general insights that became important imperatives for the design process. When speaking to clients about the need for design research, I always say that traditional market research alone would never have delivered the same depth of observational information. Who would have even known to ask a focus group whether it would be okay for the toothbrush bristles to touch the top of the sink?

Design research is helping Motorola (now known as Motorola Mobility) transform its culture. After hitting some speed bumps in its design and development process (remember the Frankenstein phone that I described earlier?), Motorola is now taking customer insights seriously and leveraging those insights in the development process. Integrating customer insights into the development and decision-making process "has shifted the culture from a purely engineering-driven environment to a consumer-focused business," verified Joy Ganvik, senior director of global consumer and market insights at Motorola Mobility. I don't expect to see any more Frankenstein phones with the Motorola name on them anytime soon.

Once design researchers have gathered this information and their observations, they use left-brain analysis to sort out what they found. Similarities in behavior and attitudes are clumped together, and differences are identified. At this point in the process, designers often create a new framework for thinking about the problem. This happened at Method, the cleaning and personal-care products company discussed earlier, after someone observed detergent drips on the top of washing machines. The cleaning agent, Method researchers realized, was actually making the washing machine dirty. The company understood that there was an opportunity to fix this problem by creating a laundry detergent that would not only clean clothes but also keep the laundry room neat and tidy and free of detergent drips.

Here's another good example of design research in action. In 2006, a big Chinese sporting gear company called Li-Ning, which was founded by a former Olympic hero of the same name, needed help to compete with Western brands like Nike and Adidas that were encroaching on its turf. Li-Ning had parlayed his fame into a successful business by borrowing Western-style products and marketing. But younger customers were no longer inspired by Li-Ning's products or message, and the company's market share was eroding. Li-Ning called in Ziba, a Portland-based design firm, which launched an in-depth design research project to find out why.

"Li-Ning had great values from its founder, but they didn't know how to communicate that to the next generation of Chinese youth," Paul Backett, industrial design director at Ziba, who was involved in the project, told me. Of course, the generation of Chinese youth that Li-Ning needs to understand and sell to in order to survive in an increasingly competitive environment are those young people who are more brand-aware than their parents and also have some of their parents' disposable income.

Ziba is located half a world away from China, but it had experience with on-the-ground design research. Two dozen researchers (including Chinese and American designers) were dispatched to 10 Chinese cities, where they conducted 130 interviews and took 7,000 photographs of Chinese youth. They observed Chinese kids at home and at school and playing sports. They followed them to stores where they bought sporting goods. Such information, Backett says, "is incredibly rich stuff. You end up with insights and results that aren't driven by numbers and demographics. You get to know the people you talk to and their patterns, because you are face-to-face with them. You see sociological patterns."

Researchers discovered that Chinese youth play sports and think about sports differently than kids in America and Europe, where sports are "all about winning" and Nike's "we're number one" model, Backett points out. In China, sport is seen as the way to make friends, build relationships, and connect with their peers. Sport is much more about play and inclusion than competition and excluding those who can't play at the same level. Another insight: Chinese youth have a strong sense of national identity and are seeking an authentic Chinese sports company.

The researchers suggested that Li-Ning products should address sport as an element of play, because Chinese kids might, in one day, go biking and then play some basketball and then a little soccer. Stores should be redesigned to echo that theme, with elements such as graphics on raw concrete floors to mimic how sports are played in the streets. Fitting rooms shouldn't be hidden away at the back of the store, but brought to the middle so shoppers can interact more with their friends. "You have to immerse yourself in their world and their feelings and concerns," Backett says about the research. "There are people behind those profiles and targets."

Design research isn't only for stuff you can hold in your hand. It can also be applied to websites or software apps, which is what the

SIX

company Intuit did for its amazingly easy-to-use tax preparation software TurboTax. According to a former Intuit employer, this software was tested on real taxpaying people like you and me, who were asked to sit in front of a computer at Intuit's facilities and input tax information as researchers watched. Software makers do this all the time, because by having someone unfamiliar with the program play with it they can unearth any problems that the designers, who are too close to the nuts and bolts, might have overlooked.

This works best if the results are an honest reflection of how the product is used rather than a check-the-box laundry list. Intuit, for example, has long used usability testing to make sure people can use its software. For its tax preparation software, Intuit began doing this testing a bit out of context: Research subjects were given generic receipts to use as the basis for entering data into TurboTax. Sometime in the mid-2000s, Intuit began asking people to bring in their *own* financial information, W-2 forms, and receipts. This time the researchers spotted some alarming oversights of their previous approach. They could clearly see exactly how the software was used and how much or how little the customers could decipher. One puzzled interviewee said during the process of entering her charitable donations, "I wrote a check to my church, but the computer is asking me whether I donated 'cash' or 'items.' Where do I say I wrote a check?" The Intuit designers realized immediately they had merely repeated the confusing questions provided by the IRS instead of explaining them in simple terms that ordinary people could understand. Getting the design research right is a design challenge all its own.

In a similar way, a company called Mint goes TurboTax one better. Mint's software, which I use, aggregates information from all of my banks and financial institutions into one place and then sends the information back to me in terms that a nonfinancial guy like myself can understand. It lets me know about my expenses compared to my budget, all in real time. What's more, Mint learns my spending patterns and alerts me when it senses that I'm over my budget or tapped out. (That's when a gentle e-mail arrives noting, "You've exceeded your clothing budget this month.")

> You want the entire team on the same page, objectively, so that the marketing manager doesn't argue to keep a feature in a product for reasons of personal preference, but because a persona named Penelope wants it.

The software prompts you to think about your spending habits and savings goals, which are not often aligned, and does it in a way that's much more appealing than a spreadsheet.

Only a design research team that was looking intensely at human behavior and motivations could have developed an application that feels so intuitive and resonant with my needs (which I'm assuming matches the needs of other people without a good head for figures). Intuit was so impressed with Mint that it bought the company in 2009 for $170 million and integrated its personal-finance application into its own product lineup.

DESIGN FOR SOMEONE, BUT NOT FOR EVERYONE

It's tempting to want your products to be accepted by everyone. Logic suggests that the broadest adoption of a product will lead to more sales and a bigger market share. But the problem for a development team is this: How do you design for everyone? How do you make decisions about the right features, especially when dealing with a complex software product that can be made to do almost anything?

A better way is to define the person you are designing for (the target customer) in a way that the entire team can understand. When a clear picture of this ultimate customer is created and acknowledged by everyone involved, it is easier to reach an alignment about design details, product features, and the overall context of use. You're not excluding other types of customers, of course, but instead you are focusing on a clearly delineated persona who is a composite of real people in your target market. You want the entire team on the same page, objectively, so that the marketing manager doesn't argue to keep a feature in a product for reasons of personal preference, but because a persona named Penelope wants it. The personas we create from what we learn in our design research work best when they make Penelope tangible by describing appropriate details of the underlying goals in her life that relate to the project—for example, a name, a demanding job, her behaviors, attitudes, and uses surrounding cell phones. The made-up personas live in the parallel universe of our office and allow us to give particularity and focus to whatever it is we are designing.

We did this type of design research when creating the Intel Reader discussed in Chapter 2. Personas were particularly needed because no one in the design firm fit the profile of a potential customer. A brilliant guy from Intel, Ben Foss, who was the project leader, was dyslexic, but we couldn't design the Reader only for him. Hearing from other people with similar vision issues was the only road we could follow to know and understand people who would be using the Reader every day for a variety of different tasks.

Throughout the development of the Intel Reader, we interviewed more than 30 people who were dyslexic or who suffered from low vision or were blind. We wanted to know about their lives and problems and how they coped by devising solutions for themselves. The interviews were expanded to include teenagers

Conducting research for the Intel Reader helped the entire team develop an understanding of the needs and motivations of potential customers, and it led to important insights during the development process. *Image: LUNAR*

who had just been diagnosed with dyslexia and retirees who had recently lost their sight to macular degeneration. From this information, we shaped five personas that covered the range of disability, stage of life, occupation, and other social aspects. One of these was a dyslexic teen we named Ethan; another was James, a low-vision senior. Both Ethan and James, who were extreme cases, had needs that encompassed or exceeded everyone else in the group. At the outset, we wanted to refer to blind users as the most extreme example, but we quickly discovered that people who are blind from birth have learned to manage in the world without vision. The more demanding users are those seniors who have been dependent on their vision and then, for whatever reason, begin to lose it and must adapt to a darkening world.

Alongside these personas, we also identified scenarios in which each would be dependent on Foss's digital reader device. James, the senior, wanted to read his mail to find bills that needed to be paid and to navigate restaurant menus on his own. Ethan, the teenager, wanted digitized textbooks and class handouts to help get his homework done. At every turn, the design team turned to our imaginary Ethan and James to help make decisions about design features. How will James navigate the menus? Can he clearly identify the Select button? Is the design discrete enough for Ethan? Is it rugged enough to survive inside his backpack when he drops it on the gym floor? We needed to know whether the design expression makes James feel confident and Ethan feel cool.

The Intel Reader was launched in 2009 with a rich software user interface that satisfied the needs for both James and Ethan. James uses only two buttons on the Reader: one to take a picture and the other to hear the audio playback. Easy. But Ethan uses the full functionality of the Reader to access stored content and skip around in the content and even to transfer the audio to an MP3 file so he can "read" it later on his iPod.

What all these stories illustrate, whether they concern minivans or software or American families or Chinese youth, is that empathy and intimately knowing the customer through design research and listening are critical to the design response. Empathy is also an essential force to muster corporate will to follow through on an innovative or daring product that might veer from the traditional lineup. Without empathy, there would have been no pioneering Chrysler minivan, snazzy Li-Ning retail stores, or helpful iPhone screen lock. Without TurboTax, many Americans would be struggling on April 14 to fill out their tax forms, and without Mint they'd be sweating more each month to balance their family budget. Empathy and a human-centered ethos are the foundation of great design, because they place the *customer* first, not the marketers, analysts, or financial and engineering experts who might block that vital direct connection to the people who buy your products and services.

SUMMARY

Design starts with knowing your customers and creating a corporate culture that is keen to listen to those customers. Design research uncovers insights into their unmet wants and needs, and this knowledge leads to empathy for the customers. Designers filter this information and build it into new products and services—with an extra dose of fun and delight thrown in—to create insanely great products and services that add extra value for the customers and the company.

THE BUILDING BLOCKS

A human-centered design ethos, or empathy, is at the heart of the design process for any product or service, whether it's cutting-edge technology, a household product, or an incremental improvement to an existing product. Empathy means listening intently to customers and closely observing how they live and interact with products and services.

Design for someone, but not for everyone. Clearly define the person you are designing for, who is the target or ultimate customer. Not every product can be all things to all people.

Design research takes an anthropological view of the world. It gathers qualitative information about people to understand their behaviors and motivations, whereas traditional market research focuses on quantitative data that doesn't provide designers with the information they need.

DESIGN LIKE APPLE AGENDA

1 Does your company have a tangible understanding of customers and their motivations so that the whole team is aligned around the same goal? Chrysler managed this with its first minivan, which disrupted the car industry, while GM and Ford fumbled by assigning the minivan challenge to teams that lacked a deep understanding of the mission.

2 Can you tap into the knowledge, expertise, and experience of your staff? Would a "next bench" strategy help to define a design vision for a product or service being developed? Apple and Hewlett-Packard find this practice critical for good design.

3 How could design research augment your other research efforts? Can you create personas and life scenarios to better understand and empathize with customer needs? For challenging products, such as the Intel Reader, personas shed light on the world of customers that you might not know about.

4 Do you ask customers to help test the usability of prototypes and products? Real people are the best judge of whether

a product or service meets their needs and to ascertain what changes or improvements are necessary (e.g., Intuit's research with real taxpayers and Apple's close listening to chatter about its products).

Design with Conviction

Commit to a unique voice.

Throughout my career, I've clocked untold miles at all kinds of receptions, conferences, and cocktail parties. After a party not terribly long ago, I was thinking about how the different kinds of conversations you have at a cocktail party make a good metaphor for the ways that companies use design. Our fellow party guests are the *bore*, the *braggart*, and the *conversationalist*.

The bore is Google. You might be thinking, "Oh, I'd love to be as boring and lucrative as Google." After all, Google has an estimated 1 billion daily users and is so ubiquitous that its name has become a verb in I don't know how many languages. Yet I think of Google as the kind of boring person at a party who doesn't have much to contribute. Such people are polite and attentive, and perhaps good listeners. They look at you in a sympathetic way and say, "Tell me about *you*." You sense their lack of self-confidence while they prod you for compliments about how great they look tonight in that Brioni suit.

What is so boring about Google? As I mentioned in Chapter 5, Google drives its design process by the numbers. The company tests prototypes and variations with huge numbers of users to optimize every visual detail on every page, as when it ran tests on 41 shades of blue[1] for the HTML links on its pages. In fact,

Google runs tests to collect data to justify just about every design decision. And who can argue with that? If the right color of blue attracts 0.01 percent more of 100 million people, well, that's still a million additional clicks and a lot of money to be made.

Yet the problem with data-centered optimization is that you lose the human touch that stirs emotion with a point of view. Google is the opposite of idiosyncratic; it is like a direct democracy in its design choices. Google looks lackluster, with the clear exception of its wonderfully simple and uncluttered home page that occasionally includes an artful logo interpretation for a specific event or anniversary. Its tool aesthetic leaves an emotional depth and connection on the cutting-room floor. It's like designing by numbers: You color between the lines without asking whether the lines are where you want them.

Back at the party, there's another bore over there in the corner by the name of Gap. Gap Inc. is the San Francisco specialty retailer whose brands include middle-of-the-road Gap, higher-end Banana Republic, and lower-cost Old Navy, as well as the online brand Piperlime and a unit consisting of performance apparel for women called Athleta. Founded in 1969 with a single store in San Francisco, Gap now has 3,200 stores worldwide. But over the past few years, Gap has struggled to regain its position as the brand that once defined casual American style. The brand lost its way, *Barron's* noted at the end of 2011 due to "a surfeit of stores and a deficit of cool."[2]

To refresh its image, Gap introduced a new logo in October 2010: The iconic blue box with white lettering was replaced with a new design by Laird & Partners, which featured white lettering with a small blue box above the *p* in its name. The blowback (or, more aptly, the Internet hazing) began immediately. Gap loyalists hated the new look. But instead of retreating, the company responded by thanking fans for their "input" and asking them to share their design ideas for a new logo. "We love our version, but we'd like to see other ideas. Stay tuned for details in the next few days on this crowdsourcing project," proclaimed Gap's Facebook page.

What a nice, positive corporate sentiment. "Oh, sorry, you don't like my dress? Well, I appreciate that input! That's terrific to hear. I mean, I love this one, but please come shopping with me and we'll pick out another one." Gap retreated and scrapped the new logo, ending its brief flirtation with crowdsourcing. It was back to square one—in this case, the original square Gap logo that people were accustomed to.

Now along comes the braggart. He's the loudmouth guy over there—let's face it, it's always a guy—who shows up wearing trendy clothes and designer accessories and is more than eager to boast about his latest supposed achievement and conquest. Scratch below the surface, though, and you won't find much underneath the façade. "You just ran a marathon in record time, really?" Our braggart's name is Dell, the computer maker.

In 2009, Dell introduced a subbrand of notebook computers called Adamo (Latin for "to fall in love"), an ultrathin, sleek, and expensive rival to Apple's equally impressive MacBook Air. With its cool styling and craftsmanship, Adamo was a departure from Dell's more prosaic looking products, and it received positive reviews in the tech press. Adamo was the tank parked on Apple's front lawn. *PCWorld* magazine described the MacBook Air–Dell Adamo rivalry as a "deathmatch."[3] Guess who won? Dell withdrew Adamo from the market in 2011 as sales flagged. Despite its good looks, Adamo was way overpriced (at around $2,000) compared to MacBook Air ($1,200). But its really big problem was that Dell had showed up at the party, loud and boisterous and trailing a hot new girlfriend, but nobody believed this guy (i.e., Adamo) was anything more than a poser pretending to be a rock star.

As we stumble out of this party after a few too many tequilas, let's recount the people we met there. First the bore named Google, who listens too closely. Then the wishy-washy Gap, lacking conviction. And finally Dell, the braggart who tries showing off but can't muster long-term commitment. None of these companies is using design like Apple. Apple is at the party, too, of course, the guest who is a good listener and tells interesting stories and a joke now and then. Apple has mastered the design dialog and conversation and speaks distinctly in its own voice and with its own point of view. That voice speaks minimalism and simplicity, the lenses through which Apple makes all design decisions.

SIMPLY BEAUTIFUL

Apple's design voice arose from a singular vision espoused by Steve Jobs when the company was founded in 1976: Technology should improve people's lives and be easy to use. Technology must speak a language, he believed, that people can understand. Over decades, Jobs ensured that Apple stayed committed to this vision.

> Apple has mastered the design dialog and conversation and speaks distinctly in its own voice and with its own point of view.

Walter Isaacson, in *Steve Jobs,* suggests that Jobs's commitment to design and craftsmanship originated in part from his father, Paul, who with his wife, Clara, adopted Jobs as a baby. According to Isaacson's book, Jobs recalls how his father, who refurbished and sold used cars, would point out to his son the intricate design detailing—the lines, vents, chrome, and trim of the seats. His father also taught him the importance of carefully crafting the backs of cabinets even though they would not be seen. "He loved doing things right," Jobs says about his father. "He even cared about the look of the parts you couldn't see." At Apple, Jobs took this further, insisting that

The Dell Adamo notebook computers were beautifully designed and engineered products. This one includes a novel hinge design that raises the back of the keyboard for a more comfortable typing position.
Image: Dell

SEVEN

a good-looking computer circuit board would communicate to customers that Apple cared about how things looked and therefore how they performed. He believed that the look, the mechanics, the performance of the keyboard and mouse, and everything else mattered.

The house Jobs grew up in was also an inspiration. In the 1950s, the family moved to a subdivision in Mountain View, a town in what would later become Silicon Valley. As Isaacson points out in his book, their home was designed and built by real estate developer Joseph Eichler, who was influenced by Frank Lloyd Wright's vision of simple modern homes with glass walls and concrete slab floors. Jobs told Isaacson that this type of architecture had instilled in him "a passion for making nicely designed products for the mass market."

Jobs and his industrial design director, Jony Ive, shared the same modernist design sensibility that eschews decoration and ornamentation. The roots of modernism go back to the renowned German designer Dieter Rams, who led design at Braun from 1955 to 1997 and was a proponent of unadorned minimalism. The similarities in their work are profound. In fact, Rams said in the 2010 design documentary *Objectified* that "you find only a few companies that take design seriously, as I see it. And at the moment, that is an American company. It is Apple."[4] Rams and Ive had similar visions of what design could and should do. Rams catalogued his vision in a 1987 manifesto called "Ten Rules of Good Design," one of which is "Good design is as little design as possible."[5] Or, as we have come to know it, less is more.

Apple is committed to making each product beautiful to behold, but it is not a superfluous or superficial beauty. And its devotion to minimalism doesn't necessarily mean spartan. There can be variations in the pitch and tone of the voice that enriches the overall voice. Consider the LED that shows through the front of the MacBook casing when it is asleep. Rather than flicker or blink, the light slowly undulates, like the breathing pattern of a resting companion. Apple's design voice is about simplicity but it is also about a devotion to the details of a form, an interface, and an experience. Those details are not left to chance. A half century before the iPod appeared, the renowned midcentury modernist designer Charles Eames noted, "The details are not the details, they make the product."[6] Apple's adherence to this idea is evident in the extraordinary attention it lavishes on the details that might seem irrelevant and unimportant at other companies.

For example, you might not have noticed this, but on an Apple computer the row of connectors for the power cord, the USB cable, and the headphone jacks all line up on the same centerline. A small detail, to be sure, but this lineup illustrates an important point. It would be easy to buy stock connectors from suppliers, place them on the circuit board, and put holes in the casing wherever they needed to be to accommodate the connectors. When I was working as a mechanical engineer, I did this very thing for many products. But Apple's design voice dictates that those connectors look better and simpler and more intentional when they march along together on the same centerline.

There's an unexpected truth in the design world that extra work is needed to make products simpler.

The Apple designers are right, of course, because this positioning results in a visual clarity and discipline in symmetry. To create this symmetry, Apple buys custom electronic components so that the outside of the product appears neat and orderly. This means additional and tedious work for Apple's design and manufacturing engineers, but there's an unexpected truth in the design world that extra work is needed to make products simpler. For me, this conundrum

SEVEN

is best captured in the quirky imagination of Antoine de Saint-Exupéry who wrote in *The Little Prince*, "Perfection is achieved, not when there is nothing more to add, but when there is nothing left to take away."[7]

Tony Fadell, the former Apple executive, told me that this type of customization is the way Apple shows its commitment to its voice, regardless of the extra cost. "Apple doesn't accept the easy route," Fadell says. When Apple knows something will resonate with the customer, "then you spare no expense," whether it's new packaging or a custom connector. This conviction to a voice can't be crowdsourced or divined through focus groups. It can be achieved only if a company has a clear sense of it itself and what it wants to accomplish and a game plan to get there.

Simplicity is not just about looks; it also applies to how Apple products function. Early versions of Apple software are devoid of many useful features that competitive products pack. For example, the first versions of Apple's Keynote presentation software didn't have as many templates or animation features as Microsoft PowerPoint users have come to expect. The upside was that everything that Keynote *did* include worked as advertised and was designed exquisitely, with elegant animations and templates in the unmistakable Apple voice. Every product and service can't be all things to all people, but every product and service does support and reflect the overarching message of Apple's design expression.

The simplicity paradigm extends to the overall product strategy. Apple exerts great discipline and control over the product lineup. When Steve Jobs returned to Apple in 1997 after being ousted in a boardroom coup, he found a company with a dizzying array of products on the company roster that were being sold in a variety of channels. The simple design strategy that he had devised was breaking down and giving way to a flood-the-market concept. Once back at the helm, he interviewed all the product teams

OXO has leveraged the design language it created in this first product—the vegetable peeler—to create an entire range of products simply recognized for better ergonomics. *Image: OXO*

and then reduced the entire line to a total of four products: one portable and one desktop each for the consumer and professional markets. Returning to simplicity meant saying no, as Jobs explained to *BusinessWeek:* "We're always thinking about new markets we could enter, but it's only by saying no that you can concentrate on the things that are really important."[8]

For all my gushing about the beauty of Apple products, I must admit that sometimes they are like the rest of us: imperfect. Erring on the side simplicity can result in products that don't "listen" to people's needs and are not as powerful as many customers demand. Or it results in the iPhone's ergonomic lapse of being too slippery to hold. If you use a MacBook Pro on your lap or in bed, depending on how your wrists are positioned while typing, the front edge of the keyboard feels exceptionally sharp, even painful. The single-button mouse that Steve Jobs pursued obsessively looks simple, but it doesn't have as many time-and-movement-saving features as a two-button or three-button version. Why did Jobs insist on the single-button mouse? Because of its apparent simplicity. Call it compulsive or just plain stubborn, but to design like Apple means sometimes giving up on even sensible requirements to rigorously maintain a cohesive voice.

CREATE YOUR OWN VOICE

Creating a voice for your company doesn't mean mimicking what Apple does or replicating the distinctive look and feel of its products. The principles of austere and unfussy Bauhaus minimalism have served Apple well, because for technology products, minimalism allows the technology to shine through. It renders what might appear to be complex and complicated to a user less so because the design is clean. But the Apple voice, refined and unique as it is, is certainly not the only one out there. Don't be seduced into minimalism as the only option; companies like BMW, Ace Hotels, Nike, and OXO each do their own thing

SEVEN

with great effect. To design like Apple, you must find your own unique and differentiating design voice and apply that voice with discipline, because that is the voice customers will come to care about and to expect.

Design can sometimes take a backseat when start-ups offer a new technology or a breakthrough service. The technical innovation and the pressure to be first to market will often diminish the role of design. That strategy can work sometimes. But increasingly, companies realize that a groundbreaking technology goes only so far. They can miss out on a critical opportunity to use design to establish a brand along with their snazzy new widget. That widget might be a winning element, but it will speak even louder with a striking design voice.

To design like Apple, you must find your own unique and differentiating design voice and apply that voice with discipline.

Blake Krikorian founded a tech company called Slingbox, which sells a gadget that allows you to view your television content from anywhere with an Internet connection. The technology hadn't been available for consumers before, so Krikorian could easily have launched the product in a bland beige box, the assumption being that the technical innovation of the Slingbox alone would do the trick and find a customer base. But in a smart design move, he decided not to.

Without a huge advertising budget, Slingbox employed an unusual design by San Francisco-based fuseproject to declare its virtues—a tapered prism sporting the value proposition molded into the top of the product in a dot-pattern typeface: "My cable TV, My DVD, My Radio, Anywhere." Right out of the starting gate, Slingbox used standout design to create emotional differentiation from potential competitors, even though it was the first mover in its sector. Slingbox hit the market with a voice that proclaimed its

Sling Media worked with designers to create an iconic and memorable product—the original Slingbox. *Image: Sling Media, Inc.*

difference, not only in how it looks, but also in the technology that lets you plug into your home cable box from a faraway place.

Our friends at Method Products also embraced design early on as a way to communicate its brand message of sustainability, efficiency, and, let's face it, coolness in a category known for mostly boring and dull products from entrenched competitors like Procter & Gamble and SC Johnson.

Method founders Adam Lowry and Eric Ryan were determined to create a family of green products that were good for the planet *and* so beautiful that consumers wouldn't want to hide them away under the sink. To grab attention, they enlisted star designer Karim Rashid to rethink dishwashing liquid, a commodity product. "Adam and Eric wanted to turn the category upside down, to be completely disruptive by taking a banal object and designing it to be quite beautiful," says Joshua Handy, Method's vice president of industrial design and innovation, who at the time was working in Rashid's studio.

Rashid came up with a bottle shaped like bowling pin (which had actually originated in his design for a chess set) and the concept that the liquid would be dispensed from the bottom rather than the top when squeezed in the middle. No messy caps to fiddle with and an unusual, whimsical shape to place on the sink for everyone to see. This "iconic shape and form coupled with a unique dispensing idea," as Handy explains, changed a product that hadn't seen any innovation in decades. Launched in 2002 at Target stores, the dishwashing liquid "by Karim Rashid" was an eye-opener as well as big seller. It helped establish Method as an innovative and design-savvy company invigorating a staid category.

From the get-go, Method used design to establish a unique and beautiful brand voice. In 2003, the company followed with liquid hand soap, also designed by Rashid. Instead of a bowling pin, Rashid created a teardrop-shaped dispenser that embodied Method's design voice with its fluid sculptural forms. As Handy describes it, the hand soap was "a nice little bright aesthetic treat for the bathroom" that would eventually become Method's most successful product to date.

Every product in Method's lineup doesn't look the same, but they do share a unified design language that sets them apart and lets consumers know they are Method. "We are in so many different categories that we morph the design language to be useful and disruptive for each category," Handy says. "But the sum is always the same. People identify with it."

We have seen how computers, cell phones, and other high-tech devices can get a big bump from design, and how a more basic consumer product like hand soap can benefit, too. How about a lightbulb?

One of LUNAR's clients is a California startup called SWITCH Lighting. Founded in 2007, SWITCH developed a long-lasting, energy-efficient LED (light-emitting diode) bulb that plugs into a standard socket. This bulb features a number of winning innovations: It has the warm glow of incandescent bulbs (which are soon to disappear due to federal energy regulations) and none of the harsh chemicals and off-putting glare of many CFL bulbs (the somewhat unpopular replacements for incandescent bulbs).

That's why SWITCH's new technology needed an equally dramatic design to define it, especially at a time when many companies are investing in next-generation, environmentally friendly bulbs to satisfy energy-efficiency requirements and the demands of customers looking for more sustainable products. "We said to the designers, we have this function, so what can

SWITCH values standout design in its bulbs, packaging and marketing because it knows that a distinctive voice will help it communicate the technical advantages.
Image: LUNAR

you do with the form?" recalled Linda Elmer, the marketing manager at SWITCH. Her mandate to us was straightforward. "How can you polish it and nuance it and bring out the best of it for a finished product?"

Our designers came up with a design as striking as the new technology. It is an industrial aesthetic concept with a sculptural aluminum base and a thick glass globe mounted on top that lets you peer inside to see the circuitry and other inner workings. Sort of a retro *Star Wars* look that telegraphs exactly what the product intends to deliver: a new lighting technology for a new way of thinking about energy and the environment. "It's like holding a snow globe with a sculptural base," Elmer says, noting that design voice reflects the idea that "there hasn't been a product like this before" (and that it is worth the $35 to $40 the bulb will cost).

CONVICTION

Many clients come to me with a simple request. They obviously believe that sex sells, so they want their products to look sexy. We can do sexy, but quite honestly, that's not always the path to a successful product. The problem is not the design, but how design is regarded within the organization.

Great design (sexy or not) can be ineffectual if it is considered merely window dressing that a particular department wants to slap onto a product. This attitude often means that whatever design distinctiveness there is will be watered down along the way by engineering, manufacturing, marketing, or finance. There is always pressure to do this because of the competing entities within a company, each with its own goals and benchmarks. But creating really beautiful, ingenious, and charismatic products requires a corporate conviction that design matters, from the start, and that the company's design voice is paramount.

SEVEN

SUMMARY

To design like Apple, you must identify and define a clear, distinct, and singular voice that is used in a unified way throughout your company as the foundation of the design values and the lens through which customers see your products and services. Creating a design voice doesn't mean mimicking Apple's mantra of simplicity, but rather finding a voice that gives special meaning to your brand and represents the design values at all touch points of customer interaction.

THE BUILDING BLOCKS

Simply beautiful is Apple's commitment to simplicity and the promise that each product will be beautiful to behold, but not in a superfluous or superficial way, but one that extends beyond looks to function.

Create your own voice means establishing unique values for your company and brand that can be seen in your product and services and will always be linked to them.

Conviction is having confidence in your design voice and ensuring that all teams understand and adhere to the voice and maintain it in all products and services.

DESIGN LIKE APPLE AGENDA

1 What kind of partygoers are your products and services? The bore, the braggart, or the overbearing one? With all your products and services assembled in one room, assess how they are perceived by others and determine whether they are speaking with one commanding voice.

2 Have you defined your design voice? Can your customers recognize this voice from far away? Or are they confused by a lack of cohesion and the clutter of variations and too many choices? A design voice can be simple and minimal,

like Apple's; it can be sensually tidy, like Method's; or it can be *Portlandia* chic, like Ace Hotels.

3 Is the design voice being consistently applied from the get-go across all departments of the company? Design is not window dressing or an add-on feature. Like SWITCH's lightbulb or Method's hand soap, design is there from the beginning to define and guide the product or service from development to completion.

Design Like Apple

Bring it all together.

I attended an invitation-only party in 2011 at a swanky Palo Alto restaurant to celebrate the launch of a Silicon Valley start-up called Nest. Because the Valley is a hotbed of activity for technology and social media companies that are attracting a flood of venture capital and Wall Street investment, this promised to be yet another glitzy launch by an enterprising company of its latest tech product or service. Another Dropbox, perhaps, or the next must-have app designed by scruffy twentysomethings.

As it turned out, that was not the case at all. We had gathered at the chic Reposado restaurant to toast a company called Nest that was introducing, of all things, a new thermostat. Never before had I seen so much fanfare (or any fanfare, for that matter) over a thermostat. You know, that common household device that not many people really think about too much unless their home is either too hot or too cold, or if they want to save on their utility bill. Yet, like many things in the Valley, a place influenced by the titans of the tech industry as well as a spirit of innovation and design, both Nest the company and its thermostat were more than what they seemed to be.

For one thing, there were strong connections between Apple and the founders of Nest, both ex-Apple employees: Tony Fadell had led the iPod and iPhone development teams, and Matt Rogers had managed software development on those teams. More important, Nest's newfangled thermostat resembled Apple's products and services in a number of ways: It featured a simple, minimalist design and a commitment to detail and functionality, not only in the product but also to the context around it. Nest had managed to reimagine and innovate the thermostat focusing on how it looks, what it does, and a person's interaction with the device. In other words, Nest was aiming at that elusive goal I spoke about at the beginning of this book, the one I hear most often from executives who say to me, "We want to be the Apple of our industry."

I don't know if Nest will eventually become the Apple of the home automation industry. Yet I could clearly sense that the company was out to shake things up and that design was at the core of its mission. From what I can see, the aim is to bring simplicity and control to home automation, starting with a much-needed overhaul of the woefully outdated function of the thermostat. The Nest Learning Thermostat, as it is aptly named, remembers your daily life patterns and preferences over time, and then sets the temperature for you. It integrates information from a range of sensors—including the latest weather in your area—to inform the decisions it makes. And, of course, there's an app for that: You can control the Nest thermostat from a web browser or your iPhone. It is an innovative product surrounded by an ecosystem of service and customer-friendly smarts. Sound familiar?

Like Apple, Nest has designed every aspect of the product, service, and experience. A thermostat is duh-simple, of course, but this one accomplishes a rather complex function. The industrial design created in collaboration with California-based Bould Design is minimal and direct, not unlike Apple's single-button mouse. It's essentially a giant adjustment knob with a screen at the center.

The Nest Learning Thermostat is as simple to use as an iPod, and, over time, it learns patterns of use so it can predict the right temperature setting.
Image: Courtesy of Nest Labs, Inc.
Copyright © 2011 Dwight Eschliman.

The Nest designers reduced the thermostat to its essence, discarding everything that didn't need to be there. The website is simple, too, and easy to navigate. And, while Nest has a commitment to green ideals (a smart thermostat does help save energy), sustainability isn't the central value proposition. That's an astute strategy, because in the future the best products will attract us because they are great *as well as* because they are mindful of the environment.

I was so intrigued by the Nest thermostat that I put my name on the waiting list. On the order form, I clicked the box confirming that I had checked the wires of my existing thermostat for compatibility with the Nest Learning Thermostat. Then, like a kid at Christmas, I just waited for the package to arrive. When it did, I was disappointed to discover that, in fact, it wasn't compatible with the very modern two-stage system at my house, which Nest had not designed for. Upon further investigation, I realized why: The two-stage system gives a big bump in efficiency over older, single-stage systems. In other words, Nest had followed our Apple-like design advice by not creating a thermostat that would be all things to all people. Nest had pinpointed customers who would benefit the most and addressed those needs. Christmas will come again, and I'm eagerly awaiting the launch of the Nest Learning Thermostat 2!

To me, the Nest story is evidence that any company or organization can apply the principles of great design. The ideas and principles I have laid out in this book can take root in a company without a Steve Jobs at the helm. After all, design is more than one person or a discipline that can be learned by rote in design school. The Nest founders had worked with Jobs at Apple, and they had no doubt learned his ways and absorbed the Apple design culture, but they are branching off and following their own instincts and intuition. As I have pointed out, design is more than simply following rules: It is a way of thinking about the world and how it works. It is a mind-set and an approach to the development of products and services.

For many executives and managers, this book might be your first exposure to design and how design can change your company. I hope you are not turned off, even though your head is probably spinning with new words and concepts and promises that design can, like fairy dust sprinkled on your products, magically transform an ugly duckling into Prince Charming. I can't guarantee that, of course. I also recognize that many companies are wildly successful without taking design into account. Yet I sincerely believe that the principles I have outlined in this book can become a framework and a road map for creating products that go beyond "good enough" to "insanely great," making any measure of success even more durable. And why *not* make great products? Stores are overloaded with mediocre and boring products that customers take little notice of as they drop them into a shopping basket. Instead of the unexciting and the ordinary, why not reach for exceptional and bold products and services that will charm and delight customers and bring them coming back for more?

As you can imagine I see design everywhere, and that's not only because I am in the profession and teach design to college students who are about to enter the field. I recognize that design is more than ever a part of the conversation, not only about business and consumer goods, but also about how we live and intentionally create things that make our lives more enjoyable and the world a better place. Much of the discussion in this book concerns aesthetics and branding and designing to meet customer needs. Yet design is also playing a critical role in solving bigger problems affecting our communities, both locally and globally. That's because, at its core, design is about applying human creativity to solve problems, whether they impact a villager in Africa, a soccer mom in America, or someone striving to improve our health or nutrition or housing or environment. Apple products have charisma, but so does an affordable solar-powered lighting system that helps children who live in places with no electricity to do their schoolwork at night.

Over the years, I have worked with many executives who have sought our help at LUNAR to introduce design into their business. There have been many favorable outcomes along the way, like the Intel Reader, the Oral-B CrossAction, and the Novint Falcon, among others. But sometimes it hasn't been easy or successful. I've seen many projects that started with ambitious design goals go belly-up because of organizational inertia or the infection of an aggressive "antibody" that kills design, be it a lack of understanding about design or a reluctance to abandon traditional practices. Yet through it all I have never lost faith in the power of design and the potential it possesses to make a difference. Your company needn't become an Apple clone. It could, however, become the next iconic player in its industry, whatever that might be, using design as a blueprint and a North Star.

To help get you there, I have outlined seven principles in this book that decode what Apple does. Use these principles in your own organization to start a conversation about what is working and what isn't, and how design can play a role in the creative process.

The journey starts with this: Recognize that design makes a difference. It's the key to devising extreme emotional engagement between your company and its customers, to fashioning beautiful aesthetic expressions, to connecting to your customers with charismatic offerings, and to infusing your products with ingenuity and innovation. To embed design into the corporate culture at all levels and elevate the importance of the product as message and messenger in an age of too much information, look to the context and systems and platforms that emanate from a product or service to extend its influence. Go inside the design studio—or, better yet, turn the office into a design studio—to think out loud with collaborators about ideas and concepts and prototypes that help visualize the future with better products.

Finally, develop a sense of empathy and a human-centered design ethos that put you in touch with your customers and their needs. And, amid all that careful listening, temper the empathy with your own voice that is spoken loudly and clearly and with consistency and conviction. Design is not just fairy dust. It's hard work. Most of all, design is a prism through which to see the world and all things in it, and this and will lead you to creating insanely great products.

NOTES

ONE

1   Norman, Donald A. *Emotional Design: Why We Love or Hate Everyday Things.* New York: Basic Books, 2004.

2   Duarte, Nancy. *Resonate: Present Visual Stories That Transform Audiences.* Hoboken, New Jersey: John Wiley & Sons Inc., 2010.

3   Jobs, Steve. World Wide Developers Conference. California, 1997.

4   Cringely, Robert. *Triumph of the Nerds: The Rise of Accidental Empires.* Documentary. Oregon Public Broadcasting, 1996.

5   Cook, Tim. Goldman Sachs Technology and Internet Conference. San Francisco, California, 2010.

TWO

1   The iPod Observer, "Micorosft Confirms It Originated iPod Box Parody Video," March 13, 2006, www.ipodobserver.com/ipo/article/Microsoft_Confirms_it_Originated_iPod_Box_Parody_Video/.

2   Burlingham, Bo and Gendron, George, "The Entrepreneur of the Decade," *Inc.* magazine, April 1, 1989, www.inc.com/magazine/19890401/5602.html.

3   Burrows, Peter and Sager, Ira, "Back to the Future at Apple," *BusinessWeek*, May 25, 1998, www.businessweek.com/archives/1998/b3579156.arc.htm.

4   Jobs, Steve, "Stanford University Commencement Speech."
    Stanford University, California, 2005.

5   Isaacson, Walter. *Steve Jobs*. New York: Simon & Schuster, 2011.

6   McKim, Robert H. *Experiences in Visual Thinking*. Brooks/
    Cole Publishing Company, 1980.

7   Jobs, Steve. *Wall Street Journal*'s Technology Correspondent
    D Conference, 2010.

THREE

1   Godin, Seth. *Purple Cow: Transform Your Business
    by Being Remarkable*. New York: Portfolio, 2009.

2   Lashinsky, Adam. Inside Apple. New York: Hachette Book group,
    2012.

3   Ginsberg, Scott, "Six Prices You Shouldn't Have to Pay."
    Hello, My Name Is Blog, July 20, 2012.

4   "Tom Peters on Design," *@Issue*, Vol. 6, No. 1, Spring 2000.

5   Neil, Dan, "The 50 Worst Cars of All Time." *Time*
    magazine, 2007, www.time.com/time/specials/2007/
    article/0,28804,1658545_1658544_1658540,00.html.

6   Martin, Roger L., "Reliability vs. Validity." *BusinessWeek*, 2005,
    www.businessweek.com/innovate/content/sep2005/
    id20050929_872877.htm.

FOUR

1   "Sony promotes Kazuo Hirai to president and CEO, replacing Howard Stringer." *Wall Street Journal,* February 1, 2012.

2   "Art: The Maturing Modern." *Time* magazine, July 2, 1956.

3   "Palm, Inc. Earnings Report." September 25, 2000.

4   Barret, Victoria, "Dropbox: The Inside Story of Tech's Hottest Startup," *Forbes*, October 18, 2011, www.forbes.com/sites/victoriabarret/2011/10/18/dropbox-the-inside-story-of-techs-hottest-startup/.

5   From www.bgr.com/2011/10/03/ios-and-mac-os-x-market-shares-hit-record-highs/.

FIVE

1   Although originally introduced by Intel® Corporation, the Intel® Reader is now offered by Intel-GE Care Innovations™, a joint venture dedicated to advancing technologies such as the Reader and its expanded product family Intel-GE Care Innovations™ Achieve.

2   Isaacson, Walter. *Steve Jobs*. New York: Simon & Schuster, 2011.

3   Ibid.

4   Lashinsky, Adam. *Inside Apple*. New York: Hachette Book Group, 2012.

5   Deutschman, Alan. *The Second Coming of Steve Jobs*. New York: Broadway Books, 2000.

6   Mobility for tomorrow. 2010, http://mo-bility.com/mo/home_.html.

SIX

1   Lashinsky, Adam, "How Apple Works: Inside the World's Biggest Startup," *CNNMoney*, August 25, 2011, http://tech.fortune.cnn.com/2011/08/25/how-apple-works-inside-the-worlds-biggest-startup/.

2   Taylor III, Alex, "Iacocca's Minivan: How Chrysler Succeeded in Creating One of the Most Profitable Products of the Decade." *Fortune*, May 30, 1994.

SEVEN

1   Holson, Laura M. "Putting a Bolder Face on Google."
    New York Times, February 28, 2009.

2   Santoli, Michael. "Can The Gap Come Back?" *Barron's*,
    December 26, 2011.

3   Gladstone, Darren, "The MacBook Air-Dell Adamo Deathmatch,"
    PCWorld, April 9, 2009, www.pcworld.com/article/162909/the_
    macbook_airdell_adamo_deathmatch.html.

4   Hustwit, Gary. *Objectified*. Documentary. Plexi Productions, 2009.

5   Rams, Dieter, "Ten Principles for Good Design," Vitsoe,
    www.vitsoe.com/en/gb/about/dieterrams/gooddesign.

6   Caplan, Ralph. *Connections: The Work of Charles and Ray Eames*.
    Frederick S. Wight Art Gallery, University of California,
    Los Angeles, 1977.

7   de Saint-Exupéry, Antoine. *The Little Prince*. San Diego:
    Harcourt Brace & Company, 1943.

8   Seed of Apple's Innovation," *BusinessWeek*, October 12, 2004,
    www.businessweek.com/bwdaily/dnflash/oct2004/nf20041012_
    4018_db083.htm.

INDEX

A